The
Freedom
of Man
in
Myth

THE
FREEDOM
OF
MAN
IN
MYTH

Kees W. Bolle

Vanderbilt University Press   1968

Copyright © *1968*
Vanderbilt University Press
Nashville, Tennessee
Library of Congress Catalogue
Card Number 68–8564

Printed in the United States of America

First paperback edition, 1993
ISBN 0-8265-1248-8

In Memory of Professor Joachim Wach

Acknowledgments

I AM indebted to Miss Mary L. Vandersea and Mr. Paul L. Richards of the Brown University Library and to Ann T. Hinckley of the U.C.L.A. Research Library for the kind help they have rendered, in and above their official function as book experts. I also thank Lynn F. Lanzetta for her invaluable work in correcting and typing the first part of the manuscript, and the incisive criticism accompanying each section.

Most of all, I am grateful to my students. If this book is useful, as I hope it is, it is because of their questions and remarks. Among my former students at Brown University, I should mention especially Ellen T. Kaplan. In the second part, I owe much to Messrs. David Himrod and Edmond Krafchow, graduate students at U.C.L.A.

University of California   KEES W. BOLLE
Los Angeles

Contents

Preface to the Paperback Edition

WHEN IT first appeared in 1968, *The Freedom of Man in Myth* placed side by side the four topics of religion, humor, myth, and mysticism. Even Mircea Eliade, who favored me with the honor of being his first doctoral candidate at the University of Chicago, felt somewhat uncomfortable with the juxtapositions in my book. For him, the experience of the mystic was inseparable from, if not identical to, the "real reality" of religion; he assigned a more exalted position to mystical experience than I in my youthful enthusiasm seemed to accord it. But I did not—and still do not—think that the linkage of the four topics implies any trivialization. On the contrary, I believe that the juxtaposition itself brings us closer to our religious documents.

Although the book's first edition did not take the country by storm, it nevertheless seemed to have an impact on the solemnity that was prevalent not only among historians of religions but also among cultural anthropologists. These scholars had made so many theories and held so many assumptions that exaggerated the distance between the subject of religion and the ordinary experience of people. Here, I argued, the notion of humor—if accepted as a natural part of our existence—can open our eyes.

In the last quarter century the scholarly climate has changed somewhat. Not only has *The Freedom of Man in Myth* been read occasionally in college courses, but several serious—serious rather than solemn—writers have discovered the vital function of narration and humor in religious texts of various traditions.

The words of myths and the statements of mystics are not as obscure or illogical as many a scholar has made them out to be. Our own world is not all that different from the worlds in which these myths are uttered. Our own environs, our own modern thoughts, are not as unique as we are too often led to believe.

With this last sentence, however, I move into a discourse that the present book only intimates. For the moment, I am delighted to see the little *Freedom* appear anew, in paperback form. I hope it will help stimulate the new climate of thought still further.

This new paperback edition gives me an opportunity to correct several small errors in the original edition, for which I, rather than my publisher, should take responsibility. I thank Cathie Brettschneider of the University Press of Virginia for bringing these to my attention. Finally, I should thank two people in particular who through the years never missed an occasion to point out the need for bringing this book back into print: my friend and colleague Jerome Long of Wesleyan University and my wife and colleague Sara Denning-Bolle of Reed College.

UCLA/Reed College   KEES W. BOLLE
May 1993

Introduction

THE FIRST part of the present book speaks of myth, the second relates it to mysticism. Both subjects have filled libraries with scholarly works, for they have always intrigued scholarly minds. Both are complexes of phenomena that have enticed many to venture great theories of interpretation. No theory has gained the favor of all, and our common use of the words "mythical" and "mystical" attests to that. They can be used to express whatever the speaker wants them to express—everything from the highest praise to the lowest despisal.

This book can hardly expect to say the last word on the subject of myth and mysticism. It is neither an exhaustive study of man's myths nor of the many forms of mysticism. It only attempts to reflect on myth and mysticism coherently, with the assumption that two points are too obvious to be refuted. First, myths are literature. Second, mystics are people. Neither one of these very general facts is meant to subtract from the particularity of mythical and mystical documents, but both can be helpful to foster an understanding for them. If we take the two obvious points seriously, we may avoid much of the usual complexity and pedantry, in spite of the abundance of documents the world over. At the same time—and I hope to show that this is a great advantage for our understanding—both points may help to open our eyes for peculiarities in the world in which we ourselves live—peculiarities we are not usually inclined to associate with mystical experiences and mythical narrations. Thus the "strangeness" of myth and of mysticism does not have to be dissolved; enough endeavors in that direction have already been made and are responsible for most of the theories. Rather, some strangeness is discussed that is also quite evident in the world as we know it. The endeavors of this book then are limited, but their procedure may take away some unnecessary confusion.

The interest in mythical narratives has greatly increased in recent times. Some excellent translations and collections present myths from the most diverse sources: from ancient Egypt and India, from Eskimos and Bushmen, and from many others. Although they make fascinating reading, they are not always fully comprehensible for "modern man."

An earlier generation thought that myth was principally a thing of the past, that "advanced" Western civilization could no longer produce anything like it, or, worst of all, that myth was, in fact, the product of another kind of mind, which was dubbed "prelogical" or "primitive." Most present day specialists in ethnology or the history of religions are very hesitant to subscribe to such views. Gradually, specialists have been forced to recognize that there is a unity in the structure of man, and that the suggestion of an intellectual split which would separate one group of mankind ("the primitives") from the other (the speaker *cum suis*) is quite artificial. Powerful arguments against artificial differentiations and for a united image of man have been presented by the German ethnologist A. E. Jensen.[1] Even earlier, the American scholar Paul Radin had soberly and convincingly refuted the hypothesis of a "prelogical mentality" in a book with the telling title *Primitive Man as Philosopher*.[2] This is not the place to sum up the important work done by various ethnologists, structural linguists, structural anthropologists, and historians of religion. The important thing is that they have contributed directly or indirectly to a new and better understanding of myth. It goes without saying that this little book is not meant as a substitute for all the specialized studies, but in its own way it will reflect the changed attitude.

If it is true that we can no longer regard other nations and traditions as mentally inferior, it is still not enough to recognize their equality in a purely formal and abstract way. When we read the myths of these many others, our task is also to discover categories in our own thought and experience that disclose myth for us. The unity of all men in behavior and mind demands this from us. It is not hard to predict that for the discovery of these categories more than one attempt will be necessary. After all, it took us "Western" and "modern" people a couple of centuries to arrive

1. *Myth and Cult among Primitive Peoples*, (Chicago: University of Chicago Press, 1963). First German edition, 1951.
2. (New York: Dover, 1957). First edition, 1927.

at the overestimation of ourselves that made us consider ourselves truly advanced and logical and superior to those who were supposedly bent down by superstition and unable to use their minds. It seems to me that we shall need some time and a great deal of effort to remould our thinking. This book is intended as a modest attempt along these lines. At best, it might be seen as a practical guide in the reading, and indeed, the "tasting" of myth.

Part I MYTH

1 ❦
A
New
Interest

T H E   P R E S E N T - day interest in myth is a very recent phenomenon. Not long ago, among the great and truly "general" historians of religion, very few dealt extensively with myth. This does not mean that these historians of religion and many others did not know about myth, but they made references to it only for the sake of some other, special purpose or subject: philosophy, psychology, sociology; a developmental scheme of human consciousness.

Even Professor van der Leeuw, in his great phenomenological work, assigns only a small section to myth.[1] We

La Religion dans son essence et ses manifestations (Paris: Payot, 1948), sec. 60. (*Religion in Essence and Manifestation*, Ch. 60).

hasten to add that this section is brilliant and that throughout van der Leeuw's work most illuminating insights into our problem are revealed.[2] But then, Professor van der Leeuw is always an exception to any generalization.

Professor Wach saw in myth one of the *general* modes of religious expression. Myth was to be understood as "theoretical expression of religious experience."[3]

It was characteristic of Wach that he never abandoned his concern for general epistemological questions. He did not spend much time on the peculiarity of particular myths. Myth, for him, is in principle one of the general *given* forms of religion. As such, however, it is important: "*myth* is the *first form* of intellectual explanation of religious apprehensions."[4] Does "first" mean "first in importance" or "first in time"? Of course, one would not exclude the other, but it is clear that Wach took a certain development for granted when he spoke of myth as a primary form. This follows from his discussion of doctrine on the same page, for doctrine "grows out of the attempt to unify and systematize variant concepts." Hence, for Wach, as for most of his contemporaries, the primacy of myth is to be understood in the sense of "chronologically first" although not exclusively in this sense. The assump-

2. See esp. *De primitieve mens en de religie* (Groningen: Wolters, 1937). "Primordial Time and Final Time" in *Man and Time*, ed. Joseph Campbell, Bollingen Series XXX, III (New York: Pantheon, 1957), 324–350. "Die Bedeutung der Mythen" in *Festschrift für Alfred Bertholet*, ed. W. Baumgartner, *et al.* (Tübingen: 1950), pp. 287ff.

3. *The Comparative Study of Religions* (New York: Columbia University Press, 1958), p. 65.

4. *Types of Religious Experience* (Chicago: University of Chicago Press, 1951), p. 39.

tion of developmental stages is clear in the *Comparative Study of Religions*."[5]

The fact is that the question whether the primacy of myth had to be understood one way or the other was not posed with great urgency for Wach and others at that time. A certain developmentalism was simply taken for granted. Even in contexts which to us seem to imply the question, the question was not formulated. Indeed, we could ask now, are not myths perhaps the most crucial vessels of religion in all times? The sort of interest or proclivity necessary to raise such a question did not seem to be present then.

We may say this much—that no concerted effort was made to deal with myth as a subject central to an understanding of religion. In the worst case, this could mean a relegation of myth to a place or construct as far away from ourselves as possible: "the primitives" and "the primitive mind." In the best case, there was often still a hidden endeavor to "objectify" myth and thus take the edge off the problem as a problem *for us;* perhaps there was no absolute barrier between a primitive mentality and our own, but then at least, it was argued, there was such a thing as a "mythical" way of thinking," not less in value than our logic, but with a coherence *of its own;* we were willing to recognize the poetry of myth; yet, when reading Papua myths we spoke of a "mythopoeic" thought; or, when deciphering texts of the ancient Near Eastern or Mediterranean world and coming closer to our own historical roots, we spoke of a "mythopoeic" age. In either case, we had created a safe distance between myth and ourselves.

Small wonder that Pettazzoni still found it necessary to say

5. Pp. 67f.

as late as 1950, in a lecture to the Congress for the History of Religions:

mythology, as the science of myth, must quit its traditional anti-mythical attitude. It must be livened by the spirit of humanism, by an attitude of sympathy towards the myth as a mark and a document of our human estate.[6]

The situation has changed drastically. Earlier studies that referred to myth, even if they did not do it for religiohistorical reasons, could not remain without effect. No doubt a major factor was the work of depth psychologists. And within the circle of the History of Religions proper, there has been the increasing influence of Professor Eliade's work next to, even if often at variance with, Pettazzoni's. Among outstanding factors in changing the climate is also the comprehensive work of Professor Th. H. Gaster.[7] The change in attitude toward myth is best summarized in the work by the Dutch scholar Jan de Vries, which is devoted exclusively to the history of mythological research;[8] it is best summarized here both because of the book's subject matter and the fact of its publication, which in itself typifies the change.

The situation has changed not only among sudents of the History of Religions. The subject of myth has gained an even

6. R. Pettazzoni, *Essays on the History of Religions* (Leiden: Brill, 1954), p. 36.

7. Particularly his book on Near Eastern myth and ritual, *Thespis* (New York: Anchor, 1961 [original 1950]) and his new edition of Frazer, *The Golden Bough* (New York: Anchor, 1961 [original 1959]).

8. *Forschungsgeschichte der Mythologie* (Freiburg-München: Alber, 1961). See my review article in *History of Religions*, III, 2 (Winter, 1964), 363ff.

wider popularity; it has reached the "general public" through some recent, exquisite anthologies.[9]

Even if it were true that we "moderns" do not share in the creativity of the mythmakers (an unproven point), it is certain that we enjoy this type of literature again, no matter how fantastic it often is: descriptions of a gruesome murder in the beginning of creation; of a god being asleep and pushed around by someone else on the very first piece of earth; an egg as the origin of the universe; and so on. There certainly must be some connection between those mythmakers and ourselves. Would it be possible to locate this connection?

9. Rudolf Jockel, *Götter und Dämonen* (Darmstadt-Genf, Holle, 1953). Anne-Marie Esnoul, *et al.*, *La naissance du monde* (Sources Orientales I; Paris; Editions du Seuil, 1959). With a concluding essay by M. Eliade, "Structure et fonction du mythe cosmogonique." Charles H. Long, *Alpha, the Myths of Creation* (New York: Braziller, 1963).

2 ❦
The
Problem
of "Types"

W E W A N T to search for the sense of the cosmogonic myth, the "myth par excellence" (Eliade). At least, we want to gain some clarity about the difficulties in such a search. For this reason we started with the modest recognition that the interest in myth itself is subject to vicissitudes and fashions and that this quest has not always seemed of crucial concern to scholars.

A glance at three recent anthologies, a German, a French and an American work, will further help us orient ourselves. All three present myths; they are abundantly aware of the multitude of myths. In this respect they underline the new consensus: that the problem of myth cannot be tackled under one heading. Also, the three works are unanimous in presenting, almost without exception, myths as they are or were told traditionally. Different from many an earlier collector of myths, the collectors with the "new attitude" do not put up with excerpts or expurgations; certainly in this respect the new attitude is "scientific." The new attitude is not aprioristically, but rather empirically inclined, in Germany and France as well as in America. It seems totally at odds, for instance, with Wach's theoretical considerations.

The German work, a collection by Jockel (*Götter und Dämonen*), is the most attractive because of its wide selection of marvelous tales. It is also the biggest of the three. The absence of a theoretical bias seems indicated by the fact that it contains all sorts of myths, and not only creation myths. Moreover, the only order of the materials is geographical and thus the whole earth is covered. The book presents all major classical and primitive cultures (Egypt, Babylon-Assyria, etc.), and also present-day tribal mythologies (Siberia, North America, etc.).

By contrast, the French book (*La naissance du monde*) limits itself to cosmogonic accounts of the Near Eastern and Oriental preclassical and classical civilizations (Egypt, Sumer, Akkad, Hurrites and Hittites, Canaan, Israel, Islam, Turks and Mongols, Zoroastrianism, Indian religions, Indochina, Tibet and China). Introductions and selections are presented by specialists in each area, but a general essay on structure and function of cosmogonic myths by Professor Eliade completes the book. *La naissance* is a collection of individual efforts; nevertheless, the restriction of the materials and the concluding essay witness to a systematic intention: an effort to understand cosmogonic myths *as such*.

Alpha, the Myths of Creation, by Charles H. Long, strikes

a middle course. In view of the scope of materials, it is comparable to *Götter und Dämonen*. It presents creation myths of all peoples and epochs, of the Vedic texts and of the Navajos, of Polynesia and Babylon. Since one person, Professor Long, is responsible for both the selections and the introductions, this book goes even further than *La naissance* in systematic intent.

Granted that all these books have the merit of drawing our attention to specific myths, what do they teach us about the structure of cosmogony? There is no scholarship totally devoid of theory. This is also true for the least theoretically inclined work, *Götter und Dämonen*. Consequently the editor felt it necessary to add an introduction. It is of the utmost brevity (four pages), but in these four pages a typology of myth is ventured. What is listed as "types" on p. 11 is very simple: *theogonies* deal with the origin and vicissitudes of the gods; *cosmogonic myths* with the origin of the world; *cosmologies* are said to explain the world (they are "welterklärend") and recount the development of the world and its parts, qualities and peculiarities. (Examples of cosmologies are vegetation and astral myths.) Jockel concludes the list with *soteriologies*, *eschatologies*, and *etiologies*. The etiological myths "interpret [deuten] peculiarities in creation, e.g., peculiar formations of stone or uncommon forms of plants and animals." The paragraph ends most meaningfully with the remark: "Pure types of myth are rare."

How could it be otherwise? What is called "cosmogonic" by Jockel (dealing with the origin of the world) can hardly be separated from "cosmological" (explaining the world, recounting its peculiarities, etc.). Again, there is no reason why some cosmogonic myths could not be etiological at the same time. The word "etiological" is commonly used as bearing on the *cause* of a certain state of things. But especially if it is used in a somewhat wider sense, as by Jockel ("interpreting," *deutend*), in many cases all types are bound to flow together. For instance, the famous Akkadian creation story (*Enuma elish*) can, with equal right, be called theogonic, cosmogonic, cosmological and etiological; it tells how the accepted gods came to power, rallied around Marduk; it presents the drama of the world's origin; it also tells about the world's basic parts, qualities, and peculiarities; it certainly interprets man's life by depicting him as fashioned from the blood of Kingu, the rebellious god, and as designed to serve the gods.

The trouble with all these words that are meant to indicate "types" of myth is that they show their ambivalence when they are put side by side. On the one hand, they are very logical—logical in the sense of corresponding to our habits of thought; we distinguish between the gods and the world, as if distinguishing between metaphysics and physics; we assign a special place to logic, to examine formally the coherence or incoherence of things. "Etiological" especially points to a mental attitude rather than anything else. A myth is "etiological" only because of its (real or imputed) intention to *explain*. On the other hand, some of the words used for "types" refer really to concrete motifs of myths. One can dub a myth soteriological only on the basis of its contents: some superhuman figure brings about weal or salvation for man.

Granted that "etiology" and "soteriology" are extreme examples in the list, they show how difficult it is to arrive at a tenable typology. When employed in the study of myth, each "type" seems bound to suffer from the ambiguity between (abstract) mental constructs and (concrete) literary motifs.

In *Götter und Dämonen*, the difficulty is not surmounted, either in the words preceding each subdivision or in the general introduction. Is a solution perhaps impossible? Or is there something about the principle underlying the all-inclusive geographical division that evades the question?

There is something frightening in the goodwill the editor displays on p. 9. He reminds us that myths "are not merely edifying and interesting stories; rather, they have a profound inner validity." He points out that they are of venerable antiquity and says, in summary: "The meaning of myths is that—within their culture—they are the mediators of religious truth and knowledge and that as such they are esteemed."

Is there not perhaps a little left of the spook of objectification in these three words: "within their culture"? No one doubts that myths are important *in their culture*. But to seek their meaning in view of that fact ignores the fundamental problem of religious meaning, even if the presence of such meaning is acknowledged *in a formal manner*. This procedure reminds us too much of the older view that myths are feeble and strange answers to man's questions about his universe and himself, which questions differ from one period to another and from culture to culture. Then, myth is still no more than a collection of "merely edifying and interesting stories."

All these considerations belong to our search for the sense of the cosmogonic myth; they are no attack on *Götter und Dämonen*. Dr. Jockel's work is still a most appealing collection. The problems arise from the material: myths. Dr. Jockel underlines the problem by enumerating a number of mythical motifs (such as cosmic renewal, deluge, magic flight), immediately following the "types."

Indeed, even when studying only one sort of myth, which can easily be identified (creation), we are faced with a multitude of motifs in the contents of each particular myth. Any method that singles out certain myths as belonging together "typically" should do so only because of what is demonstrably the intentionality of these myths. Of course an external scheme will not suffice. At the same time, the delineation of a type is meaningful only if it discloses myths for our understanding; not if it only assembles similar details of which the meaning is incomprehensible. Our problems then turn around three points: motifs or themes; types; our own understanding. These three are to be clearly distinguished, yet their significance is in their relationship. The principal task is to find how they should balance. Without their equilibrium something goes wrong with each of them: injustice is done to the empirical data (for example, by giving equal weight to *all* details, geographically or thematically); to the inner coherence of the materials (by establishing categories that are not ultimately related to them); to ourselves (by compiling heaps of data that are intrinsically as strange to us as were the uncompiled facts).

3 🌱
*Themes
and
Ideas*

PROFESSOR ELIADE'S approach, in all his works, is empirical. In regard to cosmogonic myths this means that he pays greatest attention to the various particular motifs.[1] Precisely because he is in search of religious meanings, he goes on to group certain motifs together and formulate types.

The cosmogonic myth is not only recognizable as a

1. Cf. especially, Ch. xii in *Traité d'histoire des religions*, (Paris: Payot, 1953) [*Patterns of Comparative Religion*]; *The Myth of the Eternal Return* (New York: Pantheon, 1954) [*Cosmos and History*]; "Kosmogonische Mythen und magische Heilungen," *Paideuma*, VI (November 1956), Heft 4, 194–204; *Myth and Reality* ("World Perspectives," Vol. 31; New York: Harper and Row, 1963).

special class because its theme is the origin of the world. Rather, it is a fundamental *type* in all mythologies because of its own meaning, which is evident in its structure and function. The importance of the *type* is manifest through the most diverse themes: the killing of a primordial monster, creation through the word, etc. In all cases, the creation myth presents a model, a prototypical account, which is presupposed in all cultic life and by all other myths. A celebrated example is the Polynesian creation myth, which is to be recited (one could almost say: applied) on many specific occasions, but always for similar beneficial purposes. For example the recital is required to implant a child in a barren womb, to gladden a somber and defeated heart, to counteract impotence and senility, to inspire man in the adversities of war.[2] Although the myth records only Io's words pronounced at the beginning of creation, it can be thus variously applied. Obviously, its creational force bears on all situations that demand a "reconstruction," which is, in effect, a creation on a smaller scale.

Such "prototypical" importance of the creation myth is borne out by many customs and narratives. Professor Eliade devoted an article to examples of the use of cosmogonic myths for therapeutic purposes.[3] It becomes quite clear in this article that he has gone beyond the mere registration of motifs. One example will illustrate this.

Among the Na-khi (Southeast China) the shaman is able to cure people when they have been stricken with disease. Diseases are caused by the *nāgas*, "serpents," the primordial enemies of the

2. The exposition by a Polynesian spokesman has been recorded by E. S. C. Handy, *Polynesian Religion* (Honolulu, 1927), pp. 10–11. Quoted and discussed by Eliade, *La naissance*, pp. 472ff., *Traité*, pp. 350–351.

3. "Kosmogonische Mythen . . ."

people. Why is the shaman able to cure the sick? Because the primordial shaman, Dto-mba, with the help of the mythical bird Garuḍa, fought and conquered the *nāgas* in mythical time. It is essential for the cure that the myth of Garuḍa's origin be told by the officiating shaman: magic eggs were hatched out on the holy mountain Kailāsa; Garuḍa was born and descended to protect the people from the serpents. It is noteworthy that this therapeutical recitation is preceded by a song that gives a succinct account of the creation. This song recalls the time at which *nāgas* and dragons came into being, when the sky appeared, sun, moon, and planets were brought forth.[4]

The important point is that the therapeutical myth is not itself a creation account, although meaningfully related to it. Even the realization that medicinal herbs and therapeutic acts are frequently related to the cosmogony cannot change the fact that the fundamental importance of the creation mythology cannot be proved by statistics; too many accounts of religious therapeutics do not mention the creation. A procedure other than that of the thematic statistician is needed.

In addition to the example quoted from Professor Eliade's article, many others could be mentioned telling us of myths other than the creation myth that are used to restore health, endow one with specific powers, etc. They all have in common, however, that they speak of *beginnings,* as in the case of Garuḍa's nativity myth. We are told how an old Norse poet whose creativity was exhausted was to recall how the heavenly and indeed first poet Odin acquired

4. J. F. Rock, *The Na-khi Nāga Cult and Related Ceremonies* (2 vols.; Rome, 1952), I, 9f., 97 [quoted in Eliade, "Kosmogonische Mythen . . .," pp. 198–199].

his "scaldic mead."[5] The wounded Väinämöinen, the hero of the Finnish epic, is healed; essential to the cure is the recitation of the myth of that which inflicted the wounds—the myth of the origin of iron.[6]

The problem that we have indicated here has been illuminated by an exchange of views between Pettazzoni and Eliade. Most succinctly the question is, which topic should receive more attention, the myths of creation or the myths of origin?[7] Thus formulated, the question seems incomplete. For does it not imply another question: what principle should guide a typology? Although both authors were no doubt fully aware of it, the latter question was not clearly posed during that brief discussion, and a certain ambiguity was inevitable, at least in the earlier essay by Pettazzoni. The problem of the two questions and the related problem of ambiguity cannot be imputed to the doings of some scholar. Like the problems we met before, they are proper to the study of myth itself. Significantly, the problem of the two questions is reminiscent of our uncertainty as to the primacy of myth in Wach's writings: is myth the first form of religious expression historically or structurally?

In regard to our topic, the understanding of cosmogonic myths, the discussion between Pettazzoni and Eliade is most instructive. The former is more occupied with questions of his-

5. A. G. van Hamel, "The Conception of Fate in Early Teutonic and Celtic Religion," *Saga-Book of the Viking Society* (Coventry, England, 1928–36), XI, 209, quoted in G. van der Leeuw, "Primordial Time," pp. 331–332.

6. W. F. Kirby (trans.), *Kalevala: The Land of Heroes*, (2 vols.; London: Dent [Everyman's Library], 1961), Runo IX.

7. R. Pettazzoni, "Myths of Origins and Myths of Creations," in *Essays*, pp. 24–36. Eliade, in *La naissance*, pp. 490ff.

torical development; the latter is clearly more concerned with structures. Especially instructive is the realization that neither concern can exist alone. Professor Eliade once expressed this almost laconically by referring to them as two philosophical temperaments.[8] Since he added in the same place, however that the two concerns provide a necessary and most fruitful tension, we may take courage in the pursuit of the problem at hand.

According to Pettazzoni, we should see in the creation myth one of the many myths of beginnings. The myths of beginnings form the *genus,* to which creation myths as a species are subordinate.[9] "Myths of beginnings are extremely miscellaneous. In the midst of their highly differentiated morphology we find several forms that are better characterized, and of these the creation myth is one."[10] This thesis should not be taken lightly; it comes not only from one of the greatest historians of religion, but from one to whom we are indebted for a collection of myths that is unsurpassed.[11]

Pettazzoni realized quite clearly that the creation myth was among those myths that were "better characterized" in form. Yet, this realization did not lead him to see in creation accounts *basic* myths. Naturally, he recognized creation myths because of their contents, themes, and motifs. Since he saw no reason to see anything more "original" in creation than in the origins of other things (plants, customs, institutions) he was led to an elaboration

8. "History of Religions in Retrospect: 1912–62," *The Journal of Bible and Religion,* XXXI, 2 (April 1963), 107.

9. *Essays,* p. 27.

10. *Essays,* pp. 26–27.

11. *Miti e leggende* (4 vols.; Torino: Unione Tipografico Editrice Torinese, 1948–63).

on the *genus*, "beginnings," by the course of his own argument. Thus a few pages of the essay are devoted to the irrefutable interest in beginnings that is found in myth. This exposition is necessarily philosophical; it speaks of the function of the intellect, ways of human reasoning, "kausales und finales Denken," the necessity of ideologies, need for economic explanations, etc.

If anything becomes clear in these rather complex elaborations, it is Pettazzoni's insistence on the philosophical category of beginnings, in preference to the thematic category of the world's creation, to which he denies all structural pre-eminence. Unwilling to regard any particular type of myth as basic, he has to attribute extraordinary importance to a *form of thought* that is preoccupied with origins. In terms of earlier discussion, this means that all myths take a similar turn—an etiological one. This brings out once more the difficulty of doing justice simultaneously to the contents of particular myths and to their structure. Establishing their structure means necessarily attributing more weight to some myths than to others. At the same time, what is brought to a myth by the reader in order to understand it should be borne out by the myth. It seems certain that thematically no myth has a predominant concern for beginnings in general, whether "beginnings" is understood historically or rationally.

As already mentioned, Eliade's evaluation of cosmogonic myths differs from Pettazzoni's in principle:

Since the creation of the world is the creation par excellence, the cosmogony becomes paradigmatic for every category of "creation" . . . everything that appears for the first time—an animal, plant or institution—implies the existence of the world. . . . The Myths of beginnings continue and complete the cosmogonic myth. . . . That place in the cosmos which one inhabits, limited though it may be, that is the World; its "origin" and its "history" precede all other particular forms of history.[12]

It is not unlikely that Pettazzoni's objection to the creation motif as indicative of a basic type had something to do with his suspicion concerning the phenomenological approach.[13] That approach did not seem historically sound to him and, perhaps worst of all, it seemed too apologetically predisposed, too eager to prove a religious essence of the phenomena.

However this may be, is there not indeed something too specific in the word "creation myth"? Does not the very word "creation" have a biblical (and Koranic) ring to it? The word implies the figure of a creator who somehow fashions a world that is something quite apart from himself. It does not suggest, for instance, the idea of an organic process, or a birth. The chapters in Long's book *Alpha* are divided in accordance with predominant themes. It is clear that only a small number of myths can properly be called creation stories. Although the act of creating the world is by no means limited to the Jewish, Christian, and Muslim heritage, the suggestion of "creation" proper is much weaker or absent in the majority of myths.[14] The more general word "cosmogony" may be preferable.

To return to our major subject, we seem justified in concluding that we cannot dispense with typological endeavors. If we try to deal with myths and their themes as factually as possible, we

12. *La naissance*, pp. 490–491.
13. See "History and Phenomenology in the Science of Religion," in *Essays*, pp. 215–219.
14. See especially Pettazzoni, *Essays*, p. 30.

are only forced into philosophemes which are extraneous to the subject; almost unconsciously, we must decide to regard certain facts in the myths as basic, whether it is the concern for "beginnings" or something else. Taking the contents and function of myths seriously, the cosmogonic myth is indeed the most likely basic type.

It is still difficult to keep a clear distinction between *basic* and *earliest*. Eliade is no doubt right in arguing that

the first ontological speculations in the Orient and, generally, the rise of the great oriental metaphysical systems have been made possible by the fact that for millennia people believed that they knew how to make themselves contemporaries with the beginning of the World.[15]

For in their cults and rituals the cosmogonic myth could be reactualized, the world renewed. "In the final analysis, the cosmogonic systems which have been developed by the early philosophers are embedded in immemorial tradition."[16] These statements can be abundantly documented. It is sufficient to think of Śaṃkara, the great Indian system-builder who interpreted the Upaniṣads, which in turn rested on the Vedic ritual, and so on into a dim past. It is in all likelihood even correct to say that "The Ionians continued the traditions of the Orientals and the latter continued traditions of the 'Primitives.' "[17]

The greatest importance of all these observations, however, does not lie in the suggestion of a development by stages. The importance lies, rather, in the continuous and fertilizing effect of the

15. *La naissance*, p. 491.
16. *La naissance*, p. 491.
17. *Ibid.*, p. 491–492.

cosmogonic myth. One could say that as a propensity "the cosmogonic" is constitutive of man, even though its expression changes in the course of time. The study of cosmogonic myths owes its drive to this very propensity of man.

In the last few years, a feeling of uneasiness has grown concerning endeavors to look on "primitive" or "archaic" or "religious" man as being different from ourselves. We have already shown our own uneasiness with the temptation to "objectify" the problem of myth: now we may be able to see more clearly why the creation of a distance between the "mythmakers" and ourselves is a dubious undertaking. Since we can understand the great early philosophical systems as truly "embedded" in ancient mythical tradition, it becomes virtually impossible to indicate a "break." Besides, why should it be necessary to point to a "break" by which man became separated from his mythical past? There is no reason to maintain any semblance of the idea of a "primitive mentality." There is no evidence necessitating a distinction between the mythmakers and ourselves, other than in terms of motifs and emphases. The difference is only statistical; it concerns preferences for themes. The hypothesis of an essential structural difference becomes less and less defensible.

The cosmogonic myth sets the scene for all human possibilities. It would not be correct to derive its importance from the manifold applications (for example, the curing of the sick, the inspiration of the poet) for in its function it precedes all specific usage.

If it is correct to speak of a fundamental propensity of man (and for that reason of a basic myth), certainly something can be said about the contents of these myths in clearly understandable words. Eliade has dealt at length with various motifs in cosmogonic myths and is followed herein by Long. Motifs are not just literary peculiarities but they signify various intentions. Classifying and elucidating them means revealing philosophical meanings. This procedure takes us far beyond the older approach, which directly or indirectly designated all myth as a primitive form of religious expression. Positive acceptance of the mythical form as such, in its basic type, the cosmogony, makes room for a more precise investigation. This more precise investigation points to various "species" of cosmogony. These species seem often to depend in their peculiarity on economic and social constellations, or, at least, they are related to them. Yet at other times, no such "conditioning" can even be suggested. At any rate, neither Eliade nor Long would ever interpret a cosmogonic theme by economic or other "external" factors alone.[18]

For instance, ancient Babylonian mythology (like many others) knows about a primordial battle and victory over an opposing being, which is at the same time depicted as a serpent or dragon and as a female who is the source of this world's reality. Local agricultural and geographical conditions have naturally something to do with the narrative, but no single factor is enough to account fully for the myth. This myth of the dismemberment of Tiamat juxtaposes and contrasts two cosmic principles: Marduk, the heroic god, against Tiamat, the monster; as the solar god against the (primordial) waters; as light against darkness. Above all, the opposition of the two is to be understood as complementary. Thus we arrive at a more adequate understanding of a particular cosmogonic motif by means of a philosophical articulation. The theme of the dragon and a primordial fight is widespread. It is

18. "the historical conditions provide the means through which the religious sentiment expresses itself but do not create by themselves the religious sentiment." says Long in his introduction to *Alpha*, p. 21.

akin to the imagery of antagonism between a bird and a serpent. As Eliade puts it, the myth of conflict "has played a crucial role in the first systematic speculations: it shows the two opposite principles as antagonistic (Night-Day, potential-actual, Female-Male), but also as complementary."[19]

We shall not be amiss if, in anticipation of our further discussion, we notice the impossibility of the cosmogonic imagery from the point of view of ordinary human thought. The myth expresses something that can barely be expressed philosophically. No wonder that Eliade resorts to the expression of the famous mystic Cusanus: *coincidentia oppositorum*.[20]

The difficulties in our philosophical gropings do not preclude the recognition of different "ideas" or "directions of thought" in cosmogonies. It is true, though, that it would be hard to keep certain themes totally separate. In many ways, the "bloody sacrifice" exemplified in Indra's killing of the Vṛtra[21] is a parallel to the dismemberment motif. At most there is what could be called a difference in accentuation and application. It is the killing itself that is creatively effective; Indra's victorious and final blow administered to the monster is sometimes seen as tantamount to creation. Moreover, the ritual repetition of this primordial event plays a role on many occasions, for example, at the building of a new house.[22] The "creation" of a house is cultically equated to the primordial event.

In spite of its apparent usefulness, the classification of motifs in terms of "ideas" is a hazardous enterprise. Chapter II in Long's

19. *La naissance*, p. 484.
20. *La naissance*, p. 485.
21. *La naissance*, pp. 486f.
22. *La naissance*, p. 486; cf. *Le mythe de l'éternel retour*, p. 40.

collection is devoted to "world-parent myths"; it contains, among other things, the Mesopotamian myth of Marduk and Tiamat, yet the introduction to the chapter does not even mention battles or sacrifices. An Appendix is called "Creation and Sacrifice"; among the three selections included there is a version of the Hainuwele myth (from the Island of Ceram in Eastern Indonesia).[23] Hainuwele, who grew from a coconut palm, is a mythical girl through whose death and dismemberment the world of man becomes truly inhabitable and, indeed, human. The Hainuwele mythology cannot fail to impress even the most "modern" of men. The type of deity to which Hainuwele belongs and its story are curiously encouraging and optimistic.[24] The myth of Hainuwele has overtones that are quite different from the tone of "tragedy" that accompanies the creation of man in the ancient Near Eastern texts, in one of which the famous statement occurs, "When the gods created man, they allotted to him death but life they retained in their own keeping.[25]

In the Hainuwele mythology, man is not brought forth in a more or less tragic way, as a creature meant for toil and labor, but the mythical event completes his existence and transforms it for the better. Before her death men did not die, but their lives were devoid of all essentials: vegetation and nutrition and procreation. Even the coming of death is not tragic; for upon death, man will be transposed to Hainuwele's realm.

23. *Alpha*, pp. 224ff.
24. Cf. A. E. Jensen, "Prometheus und Hainuwele-Mythologem," *Anthropos*, 1963, especially p. 146: "Das Motiv der Strafe fehlt . . . völlig . . ." Cf. also Eliade, *Myth and Reality*, pp. 105f.
25. N. K. Sanders (trans.), *The Epic of Gilgamesh* (Baltimore: Penguin, 1960), p. 99.

The differences between the ideology associated with the Hainuwele mythology, and the ideology associated with the killing of the Vṛtra and of Tiamat, clamor for recognition. We have seen that the heading "dismemberment" can cover a wide range of mythical ideas concerning man. But, let us repeat it, these "ideas" are hard to pin down. Could it perhaps be that they are more closely related to the particular forms of particular myths than any tabulation of motifs could possibly show?

Among the many myths that can be thematically distinguished, only one distinct species seems to allow for a clear philosophical definition. It is the theme of the Earth Diver.[26] And yet, even though this theme seems much clearer than the ones mentioned and several others (cosmogonic egg,[27] emergence myths,[28] creation from chaos,[29] ancestors as creators[30]), we shall see that its philosophical definition leaves much to be desired.

The Earth Diver myth has many variants, but its general pattern is quite simple. As in many other cosmogonies, the opening scene presents the primordial waters. The creator sends some being, an animal, sometimes a bird, sometimes a fish, down to the bottom to bring back a little mud from which the earth can be fashioned. It is interesting that in a great many cases, particularly in Eastern Europe, the Earth Diver opposes the creator and tries successfully to exert his power over the world. Although the Earth Diver is God's helper in creation, in many cases he is called Satan. The meaning of this myth with its many variants seems quite clear:

26. *Alpha*, Chap. V; *La naissance*, pp. 487ff.
27. *Alpha*, Chap. III; *La naissance*, pp. 479ff.
28. *Alpha*, Chap. I.
29. *Alpha*, Chap. III.
30. *Alpha*, Appendix II.

The formation of the earth is not God's work alone and thus the existence of evil is accounted for. In some places a certain metaphysical and ethical dualism can be recognized, which some scholars have attributed to Iranian influences.[31] However, it should be noted that myths with the Earth Diver motif are not necessarily dualistic in this way. They may show other kinds of dualism or even lack dualism altogether. The Earth Diver motif is very widespread (occurring in various parts of Europe, Asia, and North America) and the many variants make it imperative to use philosophical keys very cautiously. For instance, in Indian and Indonesian versions the creator himself assumes an animal shape and dives for the desired mud. In North American traditions, which have much to say about two antagonistic supernatural beings, nevertheless the myth of the Earth Diver does not show any trace of such antagonism. Furthermore, in view of the varying relationships between the creator and "the other" in the various myths, clear distinctions must be made; in some cases "dualism" may be the correct word; in others the intent of the myth is merely to show that the Creator is not responsible for the evil of the world.[32]

Most interesting for our topic are the conclusions at which Eliade arrives in a longer study, which is devoted to the Earth Diver.[33] Most probably the versions in which the creator himself dives to the bottom of the ocean in the shape of an animal presents the oldest form of the myth. It is only later that the dramatic features were added which eventually led to "dualistic"

31. See La naissance, pp. 487–489.
32. La naissance, pp. 487–489.
33. "Mythologies asiatiques et folklore sud-est européen. I Le plongeon cosmogonique," RHR 1962, pp. 157–212.

developments. The dualistic interpretation of the creation was made possible by the gradual transformation of the theriomorphic helper of God into his "servant," his "companion," and finally into his "adversary."[34]

To sum up, that which for us is philosophically most recognizable (a clear form of dualism) is, in fact, late. This conclusion ought to make us very cautious in assigning philosophically conceived meanings to myths. Does this mean that we should return to speculations concerning a mythopoeic stage of mentality which had not yet grasped such philosophical constructs and concepts as "dualism"? That does not follow. After all, there are other human expressions and other pairs of opposites that may have been of equal importance and of even more relevance to man. The fact that we recognize and formulate a meaning does not imply that we perceive the original meaning of the myth. The following remark by Eliade in the same essay is disturbingly true:

Above all, we should take into consideration archaic cosmogonies and mythologies (probably of a lunar structure) which explain the world and human existence by a system of opposites and tensions and yet do not arrive at an ethical or metaphysical "dualism." The polarities which can be seen in the cosmos and in human life (day and night, high and low, chaos and creation, summer and winter, potential-manifest, male-female, birth-death, etc.) illustrate and serve as model for the periodic renewal of the universe and of life. . . .[35]

34. *Ibid.*, p. 208.
35. *Ibid.*, p. 208.

The remark is true in a disturbingly *general* sense. Every myth has a history and an origin which seems to escape our philosophical graspings. Yet, to understand without philosophy is, of course, a contradiction in terms. And the recognition of various intentions in various mythical themes is a tremendous step beyond yesterday's generalizations about mythical expression.

At the same time, it is abundantly clear that in a given number of myths we do not have to do with an equal number of complete philosophical systems which could be extracted from them. Even when myths are influenced by systematic theologies or philosophies, *it is their particular form and expression that count.* It is precisely this fact that makes mythical expression different from systematic philosophical expression. Structurally, myth precedes and surpasses philosophy in the sense that it formulates experiences more directly than philosophy. The philosopher can perhaps speak of the ambiguities of man's married life in detail. But it takes myth to tell us how God created first the earth, then man, and then woman; how he made her out of the curving of the moon, the coiling of the serpent, the embrace of the creepers, the trembling of the grass, the fragrance of the flowers, the vanity of the peacock, and various other exquisite elements; how man nevertheless complained to the creator about this woman after only a few days; how the creator took her back; how after a week the man returned to him because he had changed his mind and had remembered how lovely she was; how he left again with her—and how he came back again to be freed from her; and how the creator then merely promised that the woman would be obedient to him; how man hopelessly admitted that he could not live with her; but also, when questioned by the creator, how he had to admit in full, "Woe is me! I can neither live with her nor without her."[36]

It should be admitted that myth speaks to the imagination more clearly. Is this type of clarity, of creativity, of sensitivity lost? It is hardly possible. We are again brought back to the general question about man's propensity for the basic myth, the cosmogony.

36. Myth from Java, in P. Hambruch, *Malaïsche Märchen* (Jena, 1927), pp. 68–71; in Jockel, *Götter und Dämonen*, pp. 145–146; in Pettazzoni, *Miti e leggende* II, pp. 43–44.

4 ✿
Reformulation
of the
Question

W E   H A V E   turned from a discussion of a plurality of themes to the general question about myth, but we have learned from the thematic distinctions which are to be made.

We are convinced that the cosmogonic myth is fundamental. But we have also seen that our powers of articulation fall short when we try to do justice to the cosmogonic themes. The *particularity* and the *immediacy* of the myth do not allow for easily applicable categories. There is a certain logic to the ways that led to such concepts as "primitive mentality." If we do not want to return to such constructs and if we are right in speaking of the cosmogonic propensity of man, our task is clear. Some comprehension of the cosmogonic myth is to be arrived at; briefly, it must be a comprehension of this peculiar propensity toward the cosmogonic as *fundamental, particular,* and *immediate.* Following our discussion, "fundamental" means that the myth sets the scene for all human possibilities; "particular" indicates that the myth does not lend itself to a generalization from without; "immediate" refers to the myth's capacity to convey knowledge that is indispensable and speaks directly to the imagination.

The task may seem insuperable, for how is an understanding to emerge when it runs counter to generalization? As Pettazzoni formulated it in the essay in which he showed himself opposed to the "splendid isolation" of the creation myth: "Scientific research cannot attach itself to exceptions and can be based only upon analogies . . ." which implies some measure of generalization.[1]

The problem may be still worse since we ask for some understanding (which means a certain unity) of a subject which is itself contradictory. The cosmogony embraces not only the particular, but at the same time the general, for its basic structure implies a general validity.

The difficulty of expressing "objectively" what makes a myth is obvious. Yet, it is equally obvious that something makes it possible to read myths; something fascinates. It could not be the mere intellectual realization that "myth is the first form of intellectual explanation of religious apprehensions" without further qualification; although in reformulating the general question we find ourselves closer to Wach than we might at first have thought. The fascination of myths could certainly not be expressed in the

---

1. "Myths of Beginning and Creation Myths," *Essays,* p. 36.

gratuitous recognition of their importance "within their culture." Neither the assignment of myth to a bygone era nor the condescension of excuses for its existence in backward geographical corners can help us anymore. We have to say something that "makes sense" about those myths which used to be thought of as childish, unrealistic, irreverent, or shocking.

The task cannot be impossible. In the first place, our "modern" fascination with myth is undeniable. The re-emergence of such fascination is in harmony with the thesis put forward by Professor Eliade: "The *homo religiosus* represents the 'total man.'"[2] There is a unity in human experience which makes our fascination with the "basic myth" possible. The difficulty is only in locating this experience. In the effort to locate the myth, we do not have to be tied to one external scheme of reference. This is in accordance with good hermeneutical practice.

if we are to avoid sinking back into an obsolete "reductionism", this history of religious meanings [that is, the story of total man, his structures] must always be regarded as forming part of the history of the human spirit.[3]

The "history of religious meanings" is quite complex, and the temptation of reducing the complexity to one simple pattern should be avoided. We should proceed with caution in the examination of the cosmogonic structure, hard as it is to define. Since only some measure of unity can account for our fascination, the spell of the "basic myth" as a structure, or the "cosmogonic propensity" of man, becomes all the more binding.

2. "History of Religions and a New Humanism," *H.R.* I, 1 (Summer, 1961), 7.

3. *Ibid.*, p. 8.

We have already made a beginning with the solution of our problem. With the help of Eliade's writings we have been able to identify the three "constituents" of the cosmogonic myth. Eliade showed us its *fundamental* character and the difficulty in distinguishing the philosophical intent, which led us to recognize the *particularity* of myth. We may also add that it is Eliade who has shown what we have called *immediacy,* for he linked cosmogonic myths and orientation rites,[4] and thus emphasized that the cosmogony is related to what is clearly the most basic religious symbolism. Man "orients" himself everywhere on the face of the earth, when he pitches his camp, builds his house or a temple. The orientation symbolism, in its simplest form a square or circle with its center, has the shape of the *imago mundi,* the image of the world in its totality. The shape of the orientation imagery is not merely one item of information among many. Something *happens.* The imagery is made manifest, it presents itself, not as a concept but rather as an action which man performs or to which he submits; he becomes oriented. Man's microcosmos corresponds to the macrocosmos and this correspondence is carried out in the most "natural" cultic acts. By its very nature, the cosmogony can set the pattern for the building of a house. In a most immediate way the cosmogonic account is felt to be the prototype of man's living.

The fundamental character, the particularity and the immediacy of cosmogonic myths are clear. We see them as aspects or grasp them as constituents; but is there an avenue of understanding the cosmogonic myth in its unity?

4. *La naissance,* pp. 475ff.

5 ✣
Unconcern
for Form,
and Humor

I N M A R C H of 1964, Professor Herman Meyer of the University of Amsterdam gave a lecture at Brown University on "The Humoristic Novel from Rabelais and Cervantes to Thomas Mann and Günter Grass." Leaning on some of Jean Paul's notions concerning humor, he showed how recent works like *The Tin Drum* (*Die Blechtrommel*) cannot be written off as products of modern man's despair, but stand in a long literary tradition. Formally, there is a certain similarity in argumentation between the literary prophecies of doom concerning a modern "humorous" novel and the temptations of the historian of religion to keep the phenomenon of myth at arm's length. In view of our investigation the topic of "humor" is not too far fetched.

There are, of course, more cogent reasons to broach the subject of humor. An important one is the conspicuous role played by the extraordinary and comical in virtually all myths. As we shall see, the step from here to humor as a literary form is not hard to take.

It may not be out of place to mention another reason, a reason of scholarly tradition in the History of Religions. The importance of the Romantic Period for the study of religion is well known. We may bring to mind that in recent times it was Professor Wach in particular who dealt with problems and ideas reminiscent of the German Romantics. He dealt with such notions as "the Classical," "the Genius," "the Universal," for the sake of the understanding of religious phenomena. Thus, if we direct our attention toward the equally "romantic" concept of "humor" we do not necessarily set out on a forbidden path. However, it does mean the abandonment of hasty theories which explain only aspects or parts of our problem. The romantic notions of Wach envisaged a unified understanding of religious phenomena. Similarly, the notion of humor is to help us understand our problem, the cosmogony in its basic structure.

Writing in English, it is perhaps not superfluous to make one thing very clear, in order to avoid all misunderstanding. "Humorous" is not to be confused with "funny" or "hilarious" or any such word. Generally, the Romantics who first made humor into a topic of great interest were not so much intrigued by laughter about good jokes as they were by the profound reasons for "the smile which liberates." True humor always concerns matters of ultimate importance. What is comical in this profound way suddenly opens a vista on matters of a most incomprehensible or unacceptable nature. It is not so much a matter of theory as a matter of immediate experience known to us all.

War has always been one of the greatest disasters experienced by man. In our own century, we have learned this again in most gruesome ways. Reports on horrors that defy the imagination are the order of the day. There are too many facts that can not be ignored and yet they can not be assimilated by the human mind.

Was it a mere defense mechanism that produced the innumerable jokes about the Nazi leaders during the second World War? A psychic defense mechanism had no doubt much to do with it. Yet a profound sense of humor raised the best of these jokes above the level of short-lived psychic gimmicks. The point is that no human life which is lived consciously can forever evade all unimaginable realities. Humor is not the only solution of the dilemma between unimaginable facts and the limits of our imagination, but it is an important one. It distorts the facts, but it does not distort them at random. It does not lead to a bewilderment of human consciousness, but to a new acceptance of the unimaginable, and yet inescapable, reality.

What cannot be grasped and what could lead to despair can be made to stand out boldly by a liberating exaggeration. It is exactly in the absence or in the dissolution of despair and bitterness that the truly comical account differs from satire or any of the "grosser" forms of ridicule. For what is truly comical, as Jean Paul says, "plays its poetical game with the insignificance of our mincing understanding; it makes us joyous and free."[1]

If we stop building philosophical theories about myths for a moment and listen to some cosmogonic accounts attentively, we cannot fail to notice similar smiles and, at the very least, we must notice a certain "looseness" in places where we might have ex-

---

1. "das Komische treibt mit dem Kleinen des Unverstandes sein poetisches Spiel und macht heiter und frei." Jean Paul, *Vorschule der Ästhetik*, in *Werke* (ed. Norbert Miller), V. (München: Carl Hanser Verlag, 1963), 115.

pected a set order. Before turning to the subject of humor in some detail, let us look at this "looseness" in fact and form.

Quite different from our academic procedures, the whole cosmogonic complex does not show any obsession with verifiable and logical "facts." Innumerable temples, even in the closest proximity to each other, are said to be situated in the center of the cosmos. Each is the navel of the world; they all share in the same creational imagery which is obviously felt to go beyond "factual" questions, such as: where exactly? how exactly? if the origin is here how can it be there at the same time? Together with this vagueness we find a pervading looseness in the treatment of thematic data. This "looseness" can not be accounted for sufficiently by the diversity of sources or by the history of various traditions. In Sumer, for instance, not just one deity is credited with the heroic deed of defeating the monster Asag, but two. There is one version ascribing the deed to Ninurta, another credits the goddess Inanna.[2]

In an even more abundant number of cases, the heroic deed is done by one deity, but the chaotic monsters are several. Thus, in India, the famous chapters in the Mārkaṇḍeyapurāṇa narrating the "Glory of the Goddess" present a whole sequence of battles with monsters concluded in each case with the victory of the Goddess. Each and every monster is intent on the destruction or the complete control of the world which would be tantamount to chaos. In each case, what counts most is the victory by the supreme, powerful, world-establishing deity. There is no doubt that untold millions of people have been strengthened by the account of the acts of the Goddess. In many very different ways, they have found in the narration the model of their own "existential" orientation:

2. Gaster, *Thespis,* pp. 138–139.

as the prototype of periodical sacrifices, or as the prototype of a more gnostic realization, leading to the inner experience of the Goddess in one's own "mystical body." The great variety of ways the myth is appropriated points back again to the lack of factual interest demonstrated by the myth. One could not say that this looseness developed at a late stage; rather, it is of the essence of mythical narration and appropriation.

We have seen the impossibility of finding fixed "philosophical" meanings in the battle motif. Now we want to direct our attention especially toward the looseness in the presentation of the factual data. As a rule, there is not even a single element which reminds us of a "doctrinal" interest. There is no doctrinal clinging to names and procedures: one version apparently does not exclude the other. The sort of facts which intrigue us so much are obviously not felt to be of ultimate importance. As the two Egyptologists who contributed to *La naissance du monde* express it, "it was very keenly understood that the same reality could be grasped and defined by very different myths and by various images."[3]

Is the lack of interest in "facts" a sign of "primitive mentality" which separates the ancient Egyptians (and so many others) from ourselves? On the contrary, the disinterest in the "facts" of myth has its complement in an overwhelming interest in realities which are not exhausted by mere facts. That is to say, we are dealing with an interest which is akin to our present-day interest in myths and in the discovery of their various intentions. The question is only whether the profoundest philosophical notions are sufficient to do full justice to the expression of myth. "Humor" may be the notion that can provide an answer. Perhaps it will be a less than systematic

3. Serge Sauneron and Jean Yoyotte in *La naissance*, p. 19.

answer, but it will yield some coherence in moments which we have indicated by such words as "extraordinary," "comical," "liberating smile," "looseness." It is quite clear that the wording of specific myths is not irrelevant or random. "Humor" will be of use if it helps us to understand the specificity of myth. The cosmogonic myth tells us that which cannot be communicated in any other way. Myth is not only philosophy in a curious garb; the apparel matters.

6 ❦
Characteristics
of
Humor

J EAN PAUL distinguishes four elements or constituents of
humor.[1] His approach does not deal merely with external
categories of literature but aims at the very structure of artistic
expression. Hence we may be entitled to borrow freely from
his work in our approach to the cosmogonic myth. In listing
and illustrating our four types, we are not trying to present
precise definitions. The types or elements or constituents of
humor are not isolated from each other. We could equally
well speak of "emphases," "aspects," "qualities," or "moments"
which are clearer in one example than in another.

1. *Vorschule der Ästhetik*, see especially pp. 124–144.

Dimming the Opposites

The first type of humor dims or obliterates lines of basic distinctions, especially those between what is truly great and what is very small, what is high and what is low. That which is exalted becomes humbled and that which is humble becomes exalted by this humor. It could be said, to use a loftier expression, that high and low are found on one level *sub specie eternitatis.*

Heinrich Heine's work is a storehouse of examples of this type of humor. In his celebrated *Buch Le Grand,* immediately after having related the truly pathetic story of the drummer, le Grand, he addresses the (lady) reader:

Du sublime au ridicule il n'y a qu'un pas, Madame!

But in the final analysis, life is so deadly serious that it would be unbearable without such connection of what is pathetic and what is comical.[2]

Heine continues: "Our poets know this,"[3] and mentions some, including of course Shakespeare, the greatest of all, and the highest ideal of all Romantics. Shakespeare, Heine says, is the one who "puts the most pitiful lamentation about the world's misery in the mouth of a clown, wretchedly shaking his cap and bells."[4]

What has the whole-hearted concern of this humorous artist is not of course a short-lived stratagem to make life "more pleas-

2. Heinrich Heine, *Werke und Briefe* (ed. Hans Kaufmann) III (Berlin: Aufbau-Verlag, 1961), p. 161. "Aber das Leben ist im Grunde so fatal ernsthaft, dasz es nicht zu ertragen wäre ohne solche Verbindung des Pathetischen mit dem Komischen. Das wissen unsere Poeten."

3. *Idem.*

4. "die tödlichste Klage über den Jammer der Welt legt Shakespeare in den Mund eines Narren, während er dessen Schellenkappe ängstlich schüttelt." *Idem.*

ant"; even less is it a literary gimmick. The talent of the poets to relate the pathetic and the comical has its ground in the talent of God Himself: "They have all imitated the art of the great and first Poet who is able to practise humor most exquisitely in his world-tragedy in a thousand acts, as we can see every day. . . ."[5]

This type of humor, like the others which will be described, is no mere mockery, but has something of ultimate earnest at stake. It goes without saying that there must be something high enough to make the erasure of the line between high and low significant and suggestive. Heine creates many variations on this theme, especially when it comes to the contrast of human frailty and the longed-for "other" reality of a divine or heavenly order. It is true that Heine's irony, particularly his self-irony, adds a special flavor to his lyrical writing, but the type of humor of which we are speaking stands out in many instances. Following in his own manner the "great and first Poet," he compares (at great length) his heart with a beautiful and rare flower and then continues:

The day is still young and the sun has scarcely run half its course. Yet the fragrance of my heart has grown so strong that I become intoxicated; I no longer know where irony ceases and heaven begins: my sighs give life to the air and I myself should like to melt and flow out in sweet atoms, into the uncreated divinity. . . ."[6]

5. "Sie haben's alle dem groszen Urpoeten abgesehen, der in seiner tausendaktigen Welttragödie den Humor aufs höchste zu treiben weisz, wie wir es täglich sehen. . . ." *Idem.*

6. "Es ist noch früh am Tage, die Sonne hat kaum die Hälfte ihres Weges zurückgelegt, und mein Herz duftet schon so stark, dasz es mir betäubend zu Kopfe steigt, dasz ich nicht mehr weisz, wo die Ironie aufhört und der Himmel anfängt, dasz ich die Luft mit meinem Seufzern bevölkere und dasz ich selbst wieder zerrinnen möchte in süsze Atome, in die unerschaffene Gottheit. . . ." *Die Harzreise,* *Werke* III, p. 85

This passage shows how serious this type of humor can be. Is it by coincidence that this fading of lines shows a kinship to certain mystical experiences? Probably not. For the moment let us note that no general philosophical proposition is ventured in this type of humor by Heine or any other poet. *The obliteration of the radical split between high and low takes place only in the poetical form itself.*

There is scarcely a cosmogonic myth in which this poetical obliteration does not occur. In defiance of all experience, two opposite principles are found together or their very opposition is denied. In each case, what is said contradicts what is known by everyone who listens.

In highly sophisticated poetry, the celebrated "creation hymn" in the Ṛgveda (X 129) begins with the assertion:

> *The nonexistent then existed not, nor the existent.*
> *There was no air nor sky that is beyond it.*
> *Death then existed not, nor life immortal.*
> *Of neither night nor day was any sign.*

Such a state at the beginning of creation does not just transcend ordinary human consciousness, but nullifies it. We are not necessarily dealing with a mystical experience in each and every case. Many creation accounts only narrate and do not share in the lyrical mystic sublimity of this Vedic hymn. At the same time, it is quite obvious that the cosmogonic myth is not merely trying to explain the world and man by obliterating a distinction fundamental to man's experience. Here, as in all poetry which brings together the exalted and the lowly, we should recognize as most essential that which is most obvious: the contrast to our experience. Of course, this contrast in no way excludes philosophical meanings, but in myth the experience of the contrasts always precedes the formulation of philosophical meanings. It is only this contrast to our experience that can explain the listener's immediate attention. Quite naturally, the most common place for this "impossible" obliteration is at the beginning of the narrative. Frequently, the most conspicuous pair of opposites is obliterated by ascribing nonexistence to both. "At first there was neither earth nor sky," begins a tribal myth in Northeast India.[7] The Vedic hymn of creation went so far as to obliterate the very opposition of existence and nonexistence. Well known is the motif of a primordial proximity of sky and earth which makes the act of separation essential for the establishment of the cosmos. A tribal myth in Orissa begins:

Formerly the sky was very near the earth and everyone found it most troublesome. When the sun set it was so dark that the people could not get about. When the sun rose it was so close that many died of the heat.[8]

Such truly impossible obliteration of distinctions which are fundamental to human life reoccurs in many mystical texts. One of Boehme's profound statements says "The unground is an eternal nothing, but makes an eternal beginning as a craving. For the nothing is a craving after something."[9]

7. Long, *Alpha*, p. 105. Taken from Verrier Elwin, *Myths of the North East Frontier of India* (Calcutta: Sree Saraswaty Press, Ltd., 1958), p. 8.
8. Verrier Elwin, *Tribal Myths of Orissa* (Bombay: Oxford University Press, 1954), p. 33.
9. Jacob Boehme, *Six Theosophic Points and Other Writings*, trans. J. R. Earle, introduction by N. Berdyaev, (Ann Arbor: University of Michigan Press, 1958), p. 141.

Events taking place at the creation of man in the Kabbalah are truly remarkable. A fragment of this story in the Zohar reads:

the South took hold upon the East. The East took hold on the North, and the North awakened and opening forth, called loud to the West that he should come to him. Then the West traveled up into the N rth and came together with it, and after that the South took hold on the West, and the North and the South surrounded the Garden, being its fences. Then the East drew near to the West, and the West was gladdened and it said "Let us make man." . . .[10]

Although the account has a ring of geometrical plausibility, it is at the very least unusual to see the directions of the compass thus enlivened in approaching each other.

In India, the mythological account of the Churning of the Ocean (to which we shall return) presents in the opening scene the gods and the antigods in perfect harmony.[11] Many things must occur before the antagonism between the two becomes manifest, and only then does the God Indra come to power. Indra's ascendance to power is tantamount to the establishment of the world, and that means the world of man's experience and traditions, to which the antagonism of divine and demonic is basic, is reached. As in all creation accounts, the events leading up to the establish-

10. Gershom G. Scholem (ed.), *Zohar, the Book of Splendor, Basic Readings from the Kabbalah* (New York: Schocken Books, 1963), p. 31.

11. It is noteworthy that only in the Rāmāyaṇa version no explanation is presented for this harmony. The Mahābhārata account first shows the gods, worrying about immortality. Then Viṣṇu simply commands them (together with the demons) to churn the ocean and the process begins. (Poona ed. I, 15,10). Both the Viṣṇupurāṇa (I,9) and the Bhāgavata-purāṇa (VIII,6) tell how Viṣṇu advises the gods to make a treaty with the demons.

ment of order are given greatest attention; Indra's ascension to power fills less than one stanza.

The type of humor of which we have spoken so far is by no means limited to myths. It is noteworthy that the account of the Churning of the Ocean and many other myths are, first and foremost, brilliant narratives; we have seen other examples in texts of a mystical leaning. It still would not be correct, however, to look for mystical awareness of a unity of opposites in all cosmogonic myths. There is something in man's experience which is perhaps less profound, but certainly more widely attested. By breaking through the determination of the opposites that govern his existence, the cosmogonic account sets man free. At the very least the opposites lose their absoluteness and become relative. Let us not make the mistake of taking this type of humor too lightly. The freedom granted through it constitutes truly human life; not chaotic, but "cosmic."

This freedom can be granted in a very solemn way; in many places, the myth is narrated in a special language, used only for this purpose at the appointed hour. There are splendid examples which underline most meaningfully the profound seriousness of this humor. It may be a mere shadow of the liberating smile, yet just the same, without this smile, man's "humanness" would perish. Sometimes the cosmogonic story is recited in funeral ceremonies—literally in the face of death. We have records of a cosmogonic myth as part of the funeral rites for a deceased chief on the island of Nias (East of Sumatra).[12] Elsewhere in Indonesia, among the Ngaju Dayak on Borneo, the cosmogonic myth is again

12. Pettazzoni, *Miti e leggende*, II, 6ff. Taken from H. Sundermann, *Kleine Niassische Chrestomathie* ("Bijdragen tot de taal-, land- en volkenkunde van Nederlandsch-Indië;" XLI, (1892), 394–395.

inserted in the chants of the mortuary ritual.[13] Indonesian myths generally abound in poetic beauty and imagery; this one is no exception; it is recited in a special "solemn" language by the priests.[14] In great detail it narrates the origin of the world in general and of the Ngaju and their villages in particular, listing one by one the settlements of the ancestors.

Would it be too much to say that exactly then, when he is confronted by the sharpest possible contrast, that between life and death, man affirms his freedom? On the one hand, man is fully aware of the antagonism between life and death and of all the other inescapable oppositions (high and low, good and evil, disease and health). Man's day-to-day life is not and cannot be all there is. At the mortuary ritual it is quite evident that there is something that opposes existence. On the other hand, he knows in the myth about a totality at the outset of the cosmogony. Yet one would not be able to speak of this totality at all if it were not for the experience of opposites.

the numerous streams running one next to another were not yet spoken of, and the neighbouring kings [clan elders] were not yet mentioned.

It was in early times, in long bygone days, when no mountains rose and no hills reached up, and the black clouds were still mixed with the white. . . .[15]

Life is affirmed. In this myth it is even affirmed in great detail further on. But—does it need to be said?—systematically-logically

13. H. Schärer, *Ngaju Religion, the Conception of God among a South Borneo People* (The Hague: Nijhoff, 1963), p. 163.

14. *Ibid.*, p. 10.

15. *Ibid.*, pp. 163–164.

what is done is impossible. In the final analysis it is the expression of the myth that enables man to live and which grants him freedom to live; it sets him free from the deadening contrasts.

What is done by the Ngaju Dayak is not at all alien to other traditions—traditions in Western Protestantism, for example. In several liturgies of the Reformation a prayer is said at the interment; this is followed by the Lord's Prayer and, quite significantly, the burial service is concluded by saying the Apostolic Creed.[16] "I believe in God the Father Almighty, Creator of Heaven and Earth. . . . the resurrection of the body and the life everlasting." Hardly a stronger denial of a certainty is thinkable; hardly a stronger affirmation of an impossibility.

Myth does not deal with trifles. This is especially visible in these cases in which basic opposites are brought together. Only the most pressing existential experiences lead to such expression.

We may note in passing that there is a kinship to the experiences of unimaginable cruelty or senselessness in the "humorous" portrayals by the novelist Günter Grass. The narrator in *The Tin Drum* finds occasion to describe some of the cultural treasures of Danzig and the manner of their acquisition. No verdict is passed on the none-too-decent acquisition. Instead, the art of his description fuses the elements of human cruelty and—equally human— pious joy.

In April, 1473, the Danzig city-captains and pirates . . . succeeded . . . in capturing the [Florentine] galleon. The captain, the officers, and a considerable crew were put to the sword, while the ship and its cargo were taken to Danzig. A folding "Last Judgment" by Memling and a golden baptismal font—both commissioned by

16. G. van der Leeuw, *Liturgiek* (Nijkerk: Callenbach, n.d.), p. 219.

Tani for a church in Florence—found a home in the Marienkirche; today, as far as I know, the "Last Judgment" gladdens the Catholic eyes of Poland.[17]

Is this "merely" humorous? Whatever one's immediate reaction may be to the novelist's craft, there is no doubt that myth is indeed serious in its literary style. The opposites *must* be joined to make room for life. In this sense, but only in this sense, is what Malinowski said true, that myth is "not an idle rhapsody, not an aimless outpouring of vain imaginings, but a hard-working, extremely important cultural force."[18] It is true in the sense that myth gives a form to the freedom which makes man *man*. But this form is not "a system," although no system, economic, societal, cultural or otherwise, could function without such form. After all, we understand myths from societies and cultures quite different from our own.

Inverse Effect

The second type of humor may be called the humor of the inverse effect. To express it in a least embellished way: what is bad turns out to be or to lead to infinite bliss.

On the face of it, this type of humor seems hardly less serious than the first one. We can say only that it works in a different way than the "dimming of opposites." It is often most apparent in the clown, whose melancholy shines through the brightest colors. What is pitiable and only pitiable has a liberating effect

17. Günter Grass, *The Tin Drum* (Greenwich, Conn.: Fawcett Publications, Inc.), p. 178. Copyright © 1963 by Pantheon Books, a division of Random House, Inc.

18. "Myth in Primitive Psychology," (Original 1926) in *Magic Science and Religion* (New York: Doubleday, 1955), p. 97.

because of the way in which it is presented, and because of what we, observers or participants, already know. In no other type of humor is the real point harder to discuss and define, and yet, more accessible. What is revealed cannot be reduced to any other expression. In a flash, the disclosure is made.

A whole history of orthodox Christian theology could be presented by reviewing endeavors to determine the nature of sin. It has always been difficult for the theologian to avoid the subject, even if it could not always be his primary concern. Is sin something nonexistent? Is it a turning against God? Is it in the first place conceit or dumbness? All this and much more (or perhaps we should say: much less). It may be bad Christian theology to say that sin is a blessing. Nevertheless, were it not for sin we could not have been liberated from it. This can be realized suddenly and joyfully. Only it would be absurd to build a theological system on this momentary realization. In no systematic fashion could sin be given such full attention as in this sudden and true realization. The realization borders on the realm of the clown: gladdening in its pathos and glaring uselessness.

Such thoughts would indeed not fit theological school systems. But they do occur in mystical texts. Jacob Boehme is one of the mystics who expressed related ideas with precision, and it is not surprising that he made himself suspect in the eyes of his Lutheran brethren who relied on orthodox theological procedure. One of his treatises sets out discussing the predicaments of human reason. Reason establishes that no one has seen God and observes that worldly events are not governed by any discernible rule but are a prey to chance. Boehme's answer to the predicaments of reason makes the turn which enables the mystic to begin his quest. The answer at once sets reason within its proper limits and registers the peculiar quality of *desire* reason is inclined to overlook. This quality is nevertheless essential to reason. What would reason be without a desire for something beyond itself? It would lack all motivation for pursuing its own logical paths.

Reason is a natural life, whose ground lies in a temporal beginning and end, and cannot enter into the supernatural ground wherein God is understood. For though Reason thus views itself in this world, and its viewing finds no other ground, yet it finds in itself a desire after higher ground, wherein it might rest.

For it understands that it has proceeded from a supernatural ground, and that there must be a God who has brought it into a life and will. And it is terrified in itself at its willing of wickedness, it is ashamed of its own will, and pronounces itself wrong in the willing of evil. Even though it does wrong, yet it accuses itself, and is afraid of a judgment which it sees not. This signifies that the hidden God, who has brought himself into Nature, dwells in it and reproves it for its evil way. . . .[19]

Likewise, Nicholas of Cusa begins his famous work *On Learned Ignorance* by observing that everything in existence has an innate ability to form judgments, so that in each case its efforts and desire will not be in vain; everything can attain peace through the help of its own nature.

Somewhat comparable is the adage of Yoga study: were it not for *mokṣa* (final emancipation), *saṃsāra* (the endlessness of the world in birth and decay) would make no sense.[20] In Yoga this

19. Jacob Boehme, *Six Theosophic Points*, trans. J. R. Earle (Ann Arbor: University of Michigan Press, 1958), pp. 165–66. (My italics.)

20. For a description of this ambivalence, see M. Eliade, *Yoga, Immortality and Freedom* (New York: Pantheon, 1958), especially pp. 40–41.

insight is, in a way, more "realistic"; it is immediately related to the experience of the practitioner. The realization known through experience at the same time leads to a certain disregard for a full theoretical account of the coherence of the world and the "beyond." Lack of interest in a full theoretical world view implies a certain skepticism. With respect to the type of humor which is our proper concern here, Jean Paul has already suggested that it shows a certain kinship with skepticism. No wonder, for as we have seen, what is doubtlessly true in this type of humor does not permit insertion in a theory. In many examples of this "inverse effect," reason is bypassed in an almost turbulent manner. (The original name given to this type by Jean Paul is, *Die vernichtende oder unendliche Idee des Humors* [the destructive or infinite idea of humor]).

It will not be necessary to reiterate any more examples of primeval battles and sacrifices. By their very nature, each account of this kind contains and produces some "inverse effect." In ancient Mesopotamia, ancient India, and elsewhere the monstrous opponents of the gods provide the very material from which the cosmos is fashioned. The primordial dragon could not be entirely evil without further qualification. It is quite significant that in later Hindu tradition the monster Vṛtra was made into a Brahmin. And since the slaying of a Brahmin is the gravest of crimes, Indra himself committed a most evil act.[21] A new series of happenings was necessary to expiate Indra's guilt. It is certainly possible in this context to employ the mystical term, *coincidentia opposito-*

21. In the Bhāgavatapurāṇa (VI, 9–13) the battle takes place under the supreme wisdom and grace of Viṣṇu. The roles of hero and monster have virtually changed places: the Vṛtra displays a rare and profound wisdom. Indra is pictured as the evil Brahmin-killer.

rum. At the same time, however, we should note the inner and subtle dialectic in its immediate narrative form which cannot be replaced by something else and which has its impact on the least mystical of listeners.

In the Hindu myth as recorded in the Rāmāyaṇa, when gods and demons are together churning the ocean in their quest for Immortality, the first result of their activity is the very opposite of Immortality. The most virulent venom appears. "It was like a fire," says the myth, "the whole world of gods and demons and men was set ablaze by it." But the account does not stop with this general lamentation; the gods turn to the great god Śiva for help. Then Viṣṇu the supreme suddenly appears and (smiling!) tells Śiva what to do: the great god Śiva is entitled to the first offering and, consequently, he should take the poison and the world-establishing activity of the gods and demons can continue. The whole scene is almost "clownish" and has caused many problems for many people both in the East and West, editors and listeners, and poets who dealt with the story.

Indeed, it is particularly tempting for scholars to focus on only a single aspect. One temptation is to view the story merely as a reflection on the ideas of "sectarian" Viṣṇu-worshippers in their controversies with Śiva devotees; for is not Viṣṇu the true guide and center of the drama over and above Śiva? Next to this "ideological" interpretation, different but equally one-sided views have been suggested. It is even possible to focus on the "etiological" fragment: the swallowing of the poison turns the color of Śiva's throat into a dark blue shade, and thus the story explains a peculiar feature of the god. One of Śiva's traditional names is Nīlakaṇṭha, the Blue-necked One. (The Rāmāyaṇa does not, however, mention the change in color.)

Variants of the Rāmāyaṇa text and versions of the story differ, and the ways in which they attempt to resolve the problems differ accordingly. Some variants leave the episode out completely, or Viṣṇu's interference, so that Śiva's act becomes just one episode in a long and astonishing series of events. The (much later) Bhāgavatapurāṇa turns the story into a crown example of devotion to Viṣṇu. Viṣṇu himself does not interfere here, but Śiva drinks the poison as an act of piety, realizing that Viṣṇu will be pleased when he shows himself willing to lay down his life for others.[22]

The variety of interpretations and emendations show abundantly that the meaning of the myth is not self-evident. Disregarding the problem of the history of the text, the Rāmāyaṇa episode, as briefly summarized above and translated in full below, occurs in various authoritative manuscripts and editions and is worth our attention as an illustrious example of mythical narration. An attempt at understanding should not be limited to an etiological or ideological explanation. We should certainly carry an obsession with ideological battles too far if we saw in Viṣṇu's smile a contemptuous sneer. It is a smile. We should see rather that in a wondrous manner the world is saved from destruction at its very inception. This cosmogony is different from the victory gained by a heroic deity over a primeval monster. The divine protagonist to whom the gods flee in their panic seems to become the victim of the irresistible poison which spreads through the entire universe. He in particular seems doomed. And yet, the cosmogony goes on and reaches its end. Śiva "swallowed up . . . the terrible poison, as if it were Immortality itself . . . gods and demons together began to churn again." In only a few lines the "inverse effect" is com-

22. Bhāgavatapurāṇa (VIII, 7, 36–40).

pleted. It is clearly not a "theory" concerning gods or men or life.

Particularly in the Rāmāyaṇa story of the churning of the ocean the poison-episode speaks immediately to the listener. The reason is not hard to find. In the Rāmāyaṇa we are told in a rapid, unembellished succession about the poison, the plea of the gods to Śiva, Viṣṇu's sudden appearance, his advice, and Śiva's act; then the creative process continues. In the other versions either the throat of Śiva is given explicit attention or the theology concerning Viṣṇu is elaborated on. Hence the evocative power which is distinctly mythical is reduced.[23] It is as if a "principle" is placed between the story and the listener which makes the mythical episode either unduly trivial or heavy. Of course, the increased logical coherence should not be looked upon as a mere deterioration. Such coherence has its own outstanding value. It is certainly not a coincidence that it is the more systematized "theological" versions which appeal most to the disciplined mind of the modern scholar.[24] Yet the "inverse effect," which is harder to pin down, is no doubt more typical of myth than the "detours" of the system.

Subjective Reservedness

The third type of humor which may be useful in our discussion of myth corresponds somewhat to Jean Paul's "humoristic subjectivity" and is, no doubt, more easily demonstrable in the

23. Different from earlier text editions, the critically established text in the Poona edition of the Mahābhārata (Ādiparva, published 1933) does not contain the episode. The Viṣṇupurāṇa (IX, 81–111) and the Bhāgavatapurāṇa (VIII, 7) each in its own way, elaborate on Viṣṇu's supremacy. The latter also includes the narration of the change of Śiva's throat.

24. Jockel (pp. 101–110) retells the story adapting from both the Bhāgavatapurāṇa and the Mahābhārata. L. Renou, *Anthologie Sanskrite* (Paris: Payot, 1947), presents the Viṣṇupurāṇa version (pp. 138–140).

well-known humoristic authors than in myth. We have already noticed in passing how Heine addressed his reader personally: "Madame!" Well known in English literature is the talent of the novelist Fielding to set up imaginary discussions with the reader. Generally, this type of humor is characterized by an awareness of subjectivity which does not, however, lead to sentimentality.

The procedures of Heine and of Fielding are no doubt far from mythical composition. But the subjective type of humor is most flexible. We all know about the peculiar habit of scholars to use the pronoun "we." It is not in the literal sense of the word the *pluralis maiestatis*; rather, it is the form forced on the professor by the problem of his subjectivity. In trying to be objective he keeps turning around this subjectivity as the very center of his doings. (As we ourselves may have noticed, the present discussion is hardly an exception.) The reader or listener may look through it and at times experience a comic relief.

The subjective type of humor is expressed in forms which are quite familiar to us. A form which is at least as familiar as the professorial style and artistically much more attractive is the commentary of an author on his own work while he proceeds. The comments interrupt the story, and what happens is, in fact, the same thing that happens when the author explicitly addresses the reader. By merely speaking about the story the author turns to the reader in person, either by coming down to the reader's level or by raising the reader to his own. The effect is often comical. This form of "subjective humor" is by no means limited to the Western humorous novel.

A clear example is found in one of the many medieval tales of India. In this tale one marvel after the other takes place. A young brahmin tries to win the hand of a princess. His initial endeavors fail since only the suitor who has visited the City of Gold will be accepted by the princess. He sets out in search of that fabulous city. Finally, by the end of the tale, he marries four beauties, including his first princess, and becomes ruler of the City of Gold and lord of the aerial spirits.[25] While the most fantastic events are conjured up before the listener, the hero of the story suffers a major set-back; all his efforts seem lost. Yet he determines to reach his goal. Suddenly, at this point, the narrator himself takes the floor and assures his audience, by voicing his agreement with his hero's resolution: that "resolute men who have made great efforts will not desist before they have reached their ends."[26] The listener, fascinated by the baffling events, is at once brought back from his sympathy with the hero to the moral wisdom of the narrator.

The City of Gold is meant to entertain. The religious material of myth is obviously different. Yet in at least one respect the element of subjectivity can stand out clearly. On the one hand, the "objectivity" or authority of the material is unquestioned, much more so than in "profane" literature. But, on the other hand, there is someone who conveys this "objective" and authoritative material. It is no wonder that in religious texts a curious exchange of subjectivity and objectivity occasionally takes place. The material presented by the myth is basic, it is authoritative, "objective," but there is also the (subjective) fact that *I* report; how else would you know? The effect is, however, not just "comical"; for at stake is the very mystery of communication, made all the more profound by the authority of myth. But insofar as the subject (the narrator) is

25. J. A. B. van Buitenen (trans.), *Tales of Ancient India*, (Chicago University Press, 1959), pp. 79–101.
26. *Ibid.*, p. 95.

most deeply involved in this mystery, we are perhaps entitled to speak about this type as "subjective humor," if only we are aware of the fact that we point to a mystery.

The usual beginning of the Buddhist *sūtras* is "thus have I heard" (*evaṃ mayā śrutam*),[27] followed by the wonderful and authoritative deeds and words of the Supreme Buddha in the midst of his company of Buddhas, Bodhisattvas, and so on. It may be argued that this is a mere formalized beginning, but it is exactly these formalized words that demand attention. A certain distance is created by them, causing the authoritative words to stand out in clear relief. We may rightfully speak of a mystery, but the creation of distance is a clearly recognizable form.

The emphasis on this involvement of subjectivity in mythical narration is akin to the humor of the poet who compels the reader by means of some personal remark, by a line which is unexpectedly close to the skin, to take the whole poem seriously. It is through the suddenly revealed "subjective" side that the "objectivity" stands out, rather than the reverse, which prevails in the "more amusing" examples of subjective humor.

Somewhere Carl Sandburg wrote the playful lines:

> I write what I know on one side of the paper
> and what I don't know on the other.

The Dutch poet Hans Andreus says: "The poets know that which they do not know." Does this realization imply that poetry is nonsense? On the contrary, it discloses the peculiar validity of the poet's craft. We can now understand how the cosmogonic myth could be used at times to inspire the poet whose creative power

27. E.g., H. Kern (trans.), *Saddharmapuṇḍarīka or the Lotus of the True Law*, S.B.E. XXI (New York: Dover, 1963), 1.

had been exhausted. The poet's creative acts are indeed the re-formulation of the authoritative creative events "at the beginning." The awareness that poets subjectively "do not know" only under-lines the ("objective") knowledge as something in its own right. The whole poem by Hans Andreus runs as follows:

> *The poets know that which they do not know.*
> *They speak in their peculiar tongue;*
> *they enter into death to the beginning;*
> *they uncover life,*
> *turn to the world and see with their*
> *passionate innocence;*
> *they transform that which merely*
> *seems to be earth into earth.*[28]

Quite a number of myths use such expressions as "it is said," and "they say." And what follows is not less, but, if anything, rather more persuasive.

A Tuamotuan myth begins:

It is said that Kiho dwelt in the Void. It was said that Kiho dwelt beneath the foundations of Havaiki (in a place) which was called the Black-gleamless-realm-of-Havaiki.

28. *De dichters weten wat zij niet weten.*
    Zij spreken in hun vreemde taal;
    zij gaan de dood in tot het begin;
    zij ontdekken leven—
    en zien de wereld aan met hun
    hartstochtelijke onschuld
    en veranderen de aarde
    in de werkelijke aarde.
Hans Andreus, *Gedichten* (Amsterdam: Uitgeversmaatschappij Holland, 1958), p. 38.

Dwelling there below Kiho had no parents; he had no friend; he had no mate; there was none but him; he was the root, he was the stability.

It was said that, at that time, Kiho conversed only with his astral-double (Activating-self). His musings were within himself; his acts were performed by his Activating-self.

That place wherein Kiho dwelt was said to be the nonexistence-of-the-land; the name of that place was the Black-gleamless-realm-of-Havaiki.

It was there that Kiho dwelt; indeed, in that place he created all things whatsoever.[29]

The myth continues with a long list of Kiho's dwelling places, each with its own ringing name in the world that came to be.

The myth is recited by some person, and curiously enough, what little shines through of the element of subjectivity emphasizes the peculiarly mythical quality: that which constitutes the world. The touch of "reservedness" which comes with the mystery of subjective communication is not, of course, only a matter of such phrases as "it is said." The mystery can be glimpsed in many ways, such as the priestly chant and the special language and time for myth. All these elements point to and emphasize the fact that the myth is there, almost in spite of the people who are, nevertheless, also there.

Man's mythical propensity in regard to the mystery of communication also finds expression in religious realms which one would not immediately associate with myth. There is an eloquent

29. Frank J. Stimson, *Tuamotuan Religion*, Bernice P. Bishop Museum, Bulletin 103 (Honolulu: Bishop Museum Press, 1933), pp. 12–19. Quoted in Long, *Alpha*, p. 174.

example from a strong South Indian Vishnuite tradition. Every member of the existing Śri Vaiṣṇava communities is properly initiated by an ācārya (spiritual teacher). At set times for the purpose of cult and meditation he is to remember not only his own teacher, but the entire line of teachers of his own teacher up to Viṣṇu himself. The last three names are all names of inhabitants of Viṣṇu's celestial realm. One such recitation[30] of names runs as follows:

I am surrendering myself to him who initiated me into the knowl-edge of myself and am saluting the line of his Āchāryas; then, I am also saluting respectfully these Āchāryas, viz. the most merciful Em-berumānar who was born in Sriperumbudur, Mahā Pūrṇa (also called Periya Nambi), Āḷavandār, Maṇakkāl Nambi (also called Śrī Ramamiśra), Puṇḍarīkākshar who initiated into the secrets of Prapatti ["submission to God's grace"] Maṇakkāl Nambi, Nātha-muni, Saṭhakōpan, and Sēnaināthan (Vishvaksēnar) and Lakshmī [or Śrī, the consort of Viṣṇu] who is as sweet and dear to God as amritam [ambrosia]; and with their help I am reaching the feet of Śriyappati [husband of Śrī, i.e., God].[31]

At one end of the line is God, at the other end "I," the speaker. The recitation grasps the mystery of communication. In the very act of enumeration of the line of all teachers it establishes the relationship through which the ultimate knowledge is conveyed.

30. There are some differences in the existing Viṣṇuite traditions which are of no relevance to our context.

31. D. B. K. Rangachari, "The Sri Vaishnava Brahmans," Bulletin of the Madras Government Museum; New Series—General Section, Vol. II, Pt. 2 (Madras: Superintendent Government Press, 1931), p. 8.

The fixation or stylization of the recital should not be regarded as merely external or ceremonial; it is of the very essence of myth which, through the speaker, nevertheless speaks for itself.

Myth never argues, it does not try to convince. This is perhaps an additional reason why, with all its concrete "objective" imagery, the myth speaks so immediately to the imagination. It does not make sense to argue with the myth and say that Kiho could *not* have been living in the void, in a place not-yet-Havaiki, because the myth does not force us to accept. It just shows us. And we see.

Scripture-bound traditions, such as our own, are curiously lacking in this "subjective reservedness." No wonder, for we have made persuading almost our central concern. Islam, at least in its orthodox form, centered in scriptural revelation, is virtually without myth. Yet in our scripture-bound and conversion-minded traditions we also are gradually beginning to admit that we understand something of myth. We shall perhaps have to learn most from this subjective reservedness, this practical awareness of the mystery of communication and understanding. This type of humor (and here the word "humor" will certainly be allowed, for somewhere a smile is possible) is the opposite of fanaticism. Fanaticism is unreserved, closed, and unfortunately always misplaced, reasoning. Still more than Islam, Christianity, as "the religion of the West," can be said to be entitled to a major share of this misplaced, enforced reasoning in the history of man.

The Grotesque

"The grotesque" is the most obvious variety of humor both in the belles-lettres and in myth. No one would venture an exhaustive definition covering the grotesque in all art forms. The grotesque is unpredictable and incalculable and, consequently, hard to define.

Of Gargantua and Pantagruel we know that they were giants. Even by itself, the concept of giants is strange, but it is much stranger that Rabelais, the creator of the famous giants, withholds all information concerning ordinary measures, and instead, indicates sizes by altogether absurd means. We hear about such things as Gargantua's mare, which in size is (precisely!) like six elephants, about the fact that he carries off the bells of Notre Dame, about his capacity to eat six pilgrims in a salad without noticing them and so on.

What can be done in indicating sizes can also be done in describing locations. The patient in the mental asylum, who is the narrator in *The Tin Drum*, decides to begin his story with his grandmother sitting in a potato field. He finds it necessary to add a very precise topography. From a practical point of view it would have been sufficient, perhaps more than sufficient, if Grass had mentioned Poland, or the approximate mileage to Danzig or some such general fact. He chose instead a much more precise description of the location of Oskar's maternal grandmother. The description is so precise as to leave all general and "useful" notions far behind.

she was sitting in the heart of Kashubia, not far from Bissau but still closer to the brickworks between Ramkau and Viereck, in front of her the Brenntau highway at a point between Dirschau and Karthaus, behind her the black forest of Goldkrug; there she sat, pushing potatoes about beneath the hot ashes with the charred tip of a hazel branch.[32]

32. Günter Grass, *The Tin Drum* (Greenwich, Conn.: Fawcett Publications, 1964), p. 12.

The very precision of the topography is grotesque; the description is untranslatable into something the reader knows from elsewhere. Thus the grotesque can be particularity to the highest degree.

Like the other types of humor, the grotesque does not, as a rule, stir people to Homeric laughter. The grotesque may be hard to define, but it is always recognizable as something extraordinary and boundlessly exaggerated in measurement, and, since it is *particular* in an exaggerated way, it is always something totally by itself; at the same time it functions in a context *as if it were normal and, somehow, general.* This last point is important, for it brings to mind once more that we are dealing with something that may be "impossible," but that is not something unreal.

Next to Rabelais and Günter Grass, the name of Wallace Stevens may sound very serene. Yet he measures distance in a most extraordinary way:

> *The distance between the dark steeple*
> *And cobble ten thousand and three*
> *is more than a seven-foot inchworm*
> *Could measure by moonlight in June.*[33]

Long before Stevens, all poets have known and some have spoken of the total liberty they were allowed to take with sizes and forms. In the words of Coleridge, in his "Apologia pro sua vita":

> *The poet in his lone yet genial hour*
> *Gives to his eyes a magnifying power:*
> *Or rather he emancipates his eyes*
> *From the black shapeless accidents of size—*

33. Wallace Stevens, "Loneliness in Jersey City," *Collected Poems* (New York: Knopf, 1961), p. 210.

> In unctuous cones of kindling coal,
> Or smoke unwreathing from the pipe's trim bole,
>   His gifted ken can see
>   Phantoms of sublimity.

Hardly any myth is devoid of the grotesque. The cosmogonic myth almost always calls up images which, for all their precision, are beyond all ordinary means of representation and measurement.

Actually, the mythical formulation of the moment of the cosmogony is innately grotesque: "In the beginning," "At first," "Of old," "Before the separation of Heaven and Earth." This location in time is not the location in time as we know it. It is the location in a special time, a time-all-by-itself. It is *illud tempus* (Eliade), that particular time. In all cases, we have to do with an immeasurable measure, and a time totally outside our normal clock-system.

The suggestion that our "clocks," mechanical and insensitive instruments, have made us different from archaic man cannot be disregarded, but certainly the idea should not be carried too far. All myths witness to the fact that people have always regarded *that time* (of creation) as something special. That is to say, *that* time contrasted to their own, normal experience. The old distinction between the sacred and the profane holds true everywhere. The mere fact that our "profane time" is regulated by the clock does not make us different from people in ancient and alien cultures.

Many a myth looks upon the existing world as the end product in a series of worlds. But myth does not put this in terms of a tentative speculation. It does not shrink back from describing preceding worlds in detail.

The first world was made of lac[34] and it lasted a long while.

In a village were five Sundi brothers. They set up a liquor still and made liquor. It was very fine liquor, indeed a little too fine, for when it flowed out it burst into flames and the house caught fire and the fire spread through the world and melted the lac and the world sank down below the waters.[35]

Thus a myth of the Hill Saora.

In a myth of the Kamar the motif of the first world is linked with the motif of flood and punishment. The supreme god Bhagavan had made the world virtuous, yet the people had turned evil. It is the more tempestuous god Bhimsen who administers the punishment which brings the world to an end. The grotesqueness in the portrayal is almost on a par with the perishing world of lac. At any rate, the event is quite outside the realm of the normal physical phenomena.

Bhimsen went on alone to the place where men were living and beat them so hard that the world sank down and all the earth was covered with water.[36]

Extraordinary and exaggerated particularity to the point of being grotesque occurs quite a number of times in the story of the Churning of the Ocean. The unexpected poison that turns up during the activity of the gods is not merely one poison among many. Of course, the listener knows about poison-in-general, but the text stresses the *particularity*. It is not *a* poison, but it is *this*

34. A resinous flammable substance. Because of its qualities and relative scarcity, lac is hardly the basic material which one would associate with the creation of the world.

35. Elwin, *Tribal Myths of Orissa*, pp. 11–12.

36. *Ibid.*, p. 5.

poison with its own horrendous name, Hālāhala. It is this mighty poison, like fire, burning up the whole world of gods, demons and men. In other words, the myth is not limited to mere allegory; it does not mention poison as an illustration of the concept of destructiveness or evil in general. Something concrete, we might even say something exuberantly concrete, is central to the account. The grotesque re-emphasizes what we saw before: that myth does not argue about things but *shows* them.

The meaning of the word for immortality, *amṛta*, is quite clear. But it should be noted that the circumstances in the Churning of the Ocean in which the concept is introduced are most curious. It is in the days of yore, *illo tempore*, when the gods were together with the demons. At that time they ask themselves, "how can we be immortal (*amara*)?" They realize that it is a particular "juice" (*rasa*) that they will need. When the noun *amṛta* occurs, it appears to be the very opposite of Hālāhala, but obviously equally concrete. Śiva swallows Hālāhala as if it were *Amṛta*, Immortality. When in the end Immortality does come up, paradoxically, it ignites the world-shaking battle between demons and gods. The poet would have had all the means necessary to state the "problem of immortality," but he chose otherwise. He set before our eyes Immortality. In our own less mythical, more literary language, we could say that in the grotesque the poet of myth has a powerful instrument to create new things.

The creation of new things could hardly be better illustrated than by the long series of beings and objects which arise from the ocean during the churning by the gods. In terms of measures and numbers the grotesque is well represented. It is after a thousand years of churning that the terrible poison appears from the heads of that (particular) snake that is used as a churning utensil. For another thousand years Viṣṇu applies himself to the task of churning after having saved the enterprise from disaster, and among the new creations we find the heavenly nymphs, the *Apsaras*. Their number is given as 600,000,000. And, as if this fantastic number would not be sufficiently impressive, the narrator adds that the attendants that accompanied these heavenly nymphs were "innumerable."

The ocean produces among other things also the jewel Kaustubha. This is another example of things immeasurable by any ordinary standard; it is the name of the unique, splendid jewel known among Viṣṇu's ornaments.

One might feel inclined to suggest that poets such as the one who created the Rāmāyaṇa story of the Churning of the Ocean "went wild." Many a Sanskrit scholar would agree. MacDonell spoke of a "defective sense of proportion"[37] and suggested that one should have first-hand experience of the Indian tropics to understand such literature.[38]

It is true that no one could fail to notice the "'fantastic and exaggerated ideas'"[39] in Sanskrit literature. But it is equally evident that the grotesque is by no means restricted to the Tropics.

In mythological literature, the grotesque almost always occurs. The cosmogonic myth never measures matters in yards, feet, and inches. Just as the events of the creation take place in a time-by-itself and in a location-by-itself, the first things are fashioned by extraordinary means, sized up by extraordinary measures and accounted for by extraordinary criteria.

37. A. A. MacDonell, *A History of Sanskrit Literature* (New York: Appleton, 1900), p. 278.

38. *Ibid.*, pp. 279–80.

39. *Ibid.*, p. 279.

The reason for all this—if we are allowed to speak of a *reason* for the grotesque—is not hard to indicate, even if it is ultimately impossible to explain. "The sacred" and "the profane" are not mere concepts in a theoretical exposition. They are also *happenings* in human existence, noticeable only because of their mutual contrast and complementation. The cosmogonic myth is sacred literature and not a mere object of theoretical reflexion; it is not strangely dressed-up philosophy. It is *narrated*, it is *recited*, it *takes place*. But it takes place only by virtue of its opposite and complement—the profane happenings of human existence, the ordinary means of measuring and judging. No wonder that the grotesque speaks vividly to our imagination. It is always "striking." Above all else, through the grotesque, the liberating power of myth becomes tangible. For the myth does not merely contrast to the humdrum experiences of daily life, but it breaks through them and hence makes a new beginning when it is recited.

Obviously, the grotesque is only one aspect of myth, but this side is essential to human life. The world of man could be compared with a university which could not possibly dispense with its "absent-minded professor," the man who reckons in extraordinary measures, whose field of learning is a field all by itself, but who usually forgets about the obligations which make life "normal."

Humor and "Humor"

Need it be stressed that the "humor" of myth goes further and is, as a rule, deeper than the literary forms found in the humoristic novel? Many of our examples have already made the point. The profound humor of the great poet is much closer to the liberating quality of myth than the "humoristic novel." The obvious difference between the poet and the humoristic novelist is that the former has always been present on earth and, in a real sense, created the myths, while the latter is a late-comer in cultural history.

Yet, the humoristic novel may help considerably if modern man tries to account for his fascination by myths. Not only has the grotesque been abundantly present both in myth and in the humoristic novel since Rabelais and Cervantes, but there are similarities in structure, in spite of the difference in level.

From a certain point of view, one could see in the humoristic novel a mere "epiphenomenon" in the history of Western literature. No humoristic novel is ever as much the property of a people or national tradition as a mythology or national epic. But in each case the humoristic novel owes much of its appeal to the fact that it accompanies and indeed *plays with* the accepted, "wooden," system of morals and ideas. Cervantes plays with the accepted morale of the nobility of his time (although he does much more than that too). Henry Fielding plays with the consciously professed standards of his day. To these examples could be added many others.

The similarity to the structure of myth is manifest in the liberating effect. The best humoristic novelists do not only parody existing standards and systems, even if this is their first object. In the best cases, the liberation goes further than the parody of a particular time and cultural setting. Sancho tells Don Quixote a most romantic story about the love of a goatherd and a shepherdess. At a crucial point in the story, the shepherd and his sheep have to cross a river and because the boat is small, only one sheep can be ferried at a time. However, it is absolutely impossible for Sancho to continue the story before having narrated circumstantially about the transport of each single sheep across the water. There are three hundred sheep, and naturally Don Quixote loses count of them. Thus, because of Sancho's obsession with "empirical reality," the romantic adventure comes to an abrupt end.

Is the story of Sancho's narrative a parody of a particular philosophical system? In all likelihood, yes. But the reader of our time who has not studied the history of philosophy enjoys the account too. For he realizes with a comic relief that such a consistent realistic concern for what can be seen and verified is impossible.

In a way, such liberation in the humoristic novel is like an "after-effect." It may open our eyes for the qualities of the cosmogonic myth. But clearly, the cosmogonic myth is more. What in the humoristic novel seems to be an "after-effect," is primary in the myth. It liberates man, not only from various elementary obsessions and habituary thoughts, but sets him free from all forces which impair his human possibilities. It does what seems impossible from within the world as we know it.

7 ❦
*The Churning
of the
Ocean*

W E D I D not set out to *define* the cosmogonic myth, but
to discover its *sense* and to account for its appeal to
modern man. The notion of "humor" was our guide,
but the "proof" of our procedure can only be in an
illustration. We have purposely made many references
to one myth in particular: the Churning of the Ocean,
as it is narrated in the Rāmāyaṇa. Here, it will be
useful to present the text in full. After all, the "analysis"
of a myth is only a pedestrian expedient. Eventually,
myth is to be "tasted."

  This is not to say that there are no difficulties in
the account of the Churning of the Ocean. As we have

noticed before, there are various versions and interpretations of this myth. This means there is the problem of the history of the text. Apart from the variety of Indian sources, there is a problem in the dependence of this myth about the quest for immortality on a common Indoeuropean heritage.[1] This great historical problem is not, however, of immediate concern to us at present; it goes without saying that every myth has a history, even if we are not documented on its history at all. Our questions are related to the structure of the basic myth, the cosmogony. Because this is our major concern, we shall bypass also the historical questions about many details; a few footnotes will be added to the text to explain some of the details that are difficult to render accurately in translation.

If our pre-occupation with the concept of humor (in the most serious manner) has borne fruit, however, the sense of the myth cannot escape us. This is true even for some of the details whose individual history could fill many volumes. One such detail problem is that of the *Apsaras* who appear in innumerable Indian texts. In our myth, the heavenly nymphs called *Apsaras* arise from the ocean and for a moment their arrival seems merely to explain their name: the *Apsaras* originate in the waters, *apsu*. The play on words asks for an "etiological" explanation, but there is a playfulness which goes beyond mere etiology. For we hear of the Apsaras being rejected by the superhuman beings. Neither gods nor demons (together still forming one group at that time) choose them as their wives. This seemingly puzzling episode becomes clear when

1. See G. Dumézil, *Le festin d'immortalité* (Paris: Presses Universitaires, Annales du Musée Guimet XXXIV, 1924).

it is seen in the light of the commonly accepted traditions in the Indian Epic. Arising from the ocean, the *Apsaras* form a permanent part of the heavenly world; yet, they are, in a way, a continuation of the "chaotic." They are not chosen and belong to all. It is their belonging to all which seems entirely out of harmony with the officially sanctioned pattern of life. After all, the Indian tradition glorifies the married woman, the one who chooses and has been chosen. The *Apsaras'* behavior is different from the set forms and has a semblance of immorality. Yet their heavenliness is in no way impaired by their "immorality." As a matter of fact, their immorality is recognized and allowed and plays a great role in the Epics. They are, so to speak, a permanent feature of heaven in which the human opposites of morality-immorality are obliterated.

In terms of our myth, their arrival does not lead to a split between the gods and the demons which happens upon the arrival of the beautiful Vāruṇī, the daughter of Varuṇa, the god who has a traditional relationship to the waters. The history of Varuṇa and his daughter Vāruṇī (who in other stories is his wife) is complex; but at least this much is evident in our myth: that Vāruṇī is accepted by the gods and not by the demons. Thus the first distinction between gods and demons appears before the great battle for Immortality. Vāruṇī is related to the formation of the divine order as opposed to the powers of chaos. Thus the context in which another play on words distinguishes gods (*suras*) from demons (*asuras*), appears to be more than mere etiology and primitive etymology.

Several purposes may be served by using the Churning of the Ocean as an example. Not only does it illustrate clearly the dim-

ming of opposites, the inverse effect, and, in abundance, the
grotesque, but even with all its exuberant imagery it may convey
something of the mystery of mythical communication, which we
discussed under the heading of "subjective reservedness." It is
needless to repeat that the myth is part of the venerated book, the
Rāmāyaṇa. Moreover, the myth is told by Viśvāmitra, that is to
say, by a *guru*, a spiritual teacher, to his pupil. It is the sort of
relationship in which not merely factual, but also sacred communication takes place.

Furthermore, this story makes it very clear how difficult it is
to apply external schemes to classify myths. On the basis of an
external scheme one might even doubt whether we could speak
of a creation myth in this case. It should be borne in mind, however, that the formation of epistemological schemes depends to
quite an extent on the general structure of a religion. This holds
true for the classification of myths. Hinduism thinks much more
consistently than most other religions in terms of cycles and infinite
numbers of epochs. In addition to its long history and complexity
of sources, this accounts for the great number of cosmogonies. As
a rule, the world does not just arise; it re-arises. Since the Churning of the Ocean recounts all events which were necessary to make
the "ordinary" world governed by the god Indra possible, we are
entitled to regard the story as a cosmogonic myth in the structure
of Indian religion. The fact that a myth like this one is narrated
in the Indian Epic brings out clearly the weakness of ready-made
schemes. For, generally speaking, mythology and epic would be
regarded as distinct forms of literature.

The time of myth is always the time in which the things of
the world originated. It is a common opinion that this curious time
dimension (*illud tempus*) is the reason why myth is different from

other forms of story-telling, such as saga, legend and fairy tale. Kerényi argued, for instance, that the time of the saga differs from mythical time. The saga's time would be historical in character, or, as a rule, and more precisely, "Historical time which is stylized in accordance with virile ideals."[2] The Indian Epic makes the use of such neat categories virtually impossible. For here, turning a page, one moves from one category of time to another. In terms of "time," saga and myth often fuse. Above all, in view of our previous discussion, we are not in great need of these categories. The curious dimension of time can be seen as only one example of the "grotesque," which is itself only one of the four major aspects which we distinguished.

Last but not least, it is of pre-eminent importance that the Churning of the Ocean occurs in one of the major writings of Hinduism. The mythical concern of the Hindu Epic is one more reminder that myth must not be thought of as the exclusive property of "primitives." It is also literature, and yet more than that: myth in general, and the cosmogonic myth in particular, is to be understood as a basic dimension of human life. This dimension remains through the vicissitudes of history and enables us to recognize and understand myths in spite of their diversity, stage of development, and cultural setting.

Finally then, the myth itself. A literal translation has its shortcomings. A myth such as this one deserves a more artistic re-creation to bring out more clearly the flavor and true playfulness essential to it; it is for that reason that we add in the Appendix the poetic rendering by Griffith.[3]

2. Karl Kerényi, "Die Entstehung der Olympischen Götterfamilie" (*Paideuma* IV, 1950), p. 129.
3. Pp. 187–192.

Rāmāyaṇa I, 45, 15–44

15 In the early days, in the golden age,
There were the strong sons of Diti [Diti, mythical mother of the
Daityas, demonic enemies of the gods], and the sons of Aditi
[Aditi, mythical mother of the gods];
They were very illustrious and most virtuous and they followed
the right course of life.

16 Now the thought occurred to these great beings:
"How can we be immortal and free from old age and disease?"

17 And it occurred to those wise ones while they were thus engaged
in thought:
"When the milky ocean is churned,
Then we shall get hold of the essential juice."

18 So they decided to churn, and, being of immeasurable energy,
They used Vāsuki [the prince of serpents] as a rope in their
churning equipment,
The mountain Mandara [gigantic and holy] as churn staff, and
they began to churn.

19 A thousand years passed. Then the heads of the serpent, which
was used as churning cord, began to strike out at the mountains.
While they struck out with their fangs they were vomiting an in-
credibly potent poison.

20 Out came Hālāhala, the mighty poison.
It was like fire.

The whole world of gods and demons and men was set ablaze
   by it.

21 Then the gods were eager for protection by the Great God Śiva.
   So they went to him singing his praises and saying:
   "Save us! Save us!"

22 Thus the Lord, the great god of gods was addressed by them.
   At that moment Viṣṇu appeared at that place bearing his conch
      and his discus.

23 With a smile Viṣṇu spoke to the trident-wielder Śiva:
   "That which first of all turned up in the gods' churning,
      o best of gods,

24 That is thine, since thou, Lord,
   Art the foremost of the gods.

25 Stay here and receive the first offering, the poison, o Lord!"
   Then and there, having said this,
   Viṣṇu the supreme of gods vanished.

26 But Śiva had seen the fear of the gods
   And heard the words of the great archer Viṣṇu.
   He swallowed up Hālāhala, the terrible poison,
   As if it were Immortality itself.

27 Lord Śiva, the supreme one, left the gods;
   And gods and demons together began to churn again.

28 Then the churn staff, that most glorious mountain Mandara,
   Slipped into the underworld,

And gods and the heavenly hosts began to call on Viṣṇu with
songs of adoration.

29 "Thou art the goal of all beings, and especially of the celestials!
Thou with thy strong arms, protect us,
Thou art able to raise up the mountain!"

30 Viṣṇu heard them. He took the form of a tortoise,
Put the mountain on his back and lay down in the ocean.

31 And then Viṣṇu himself, the soul of the world, the supreme
Puruṣa,[4]
Reached out and held the top of the mountain with his hand
And began to churn in the midst of the gods.

32 After a thousand years of churning
The man of Medical Science[5] arose with his staff and his gourd;[6]
He is wholly virtuous, following the right course of life.
Thus he, Dhanvantari by name, arose, and then the heavenly
nymphs.

33 By the churning in the waters (*apsu*)
The exquisite damsels came out of that essential fluid.
Therefore they became heavenly nymphs (*apsaras*).

4. Puruṣa: "soul," "spirit," and the sacrificial victim at the first sacrifice performed by the gods at the beginning of creation (Ṛgveda X 90).
5. Literally, "the man consisting in *āyurveda*." *Āyurveda* is the traditional and
very highly esteemed Hindu science of medicine.
6. Staff and gourd (used as water jar) belong to the apparel of the ascetic.
True science is the fruit of asceticism.

34 Six hundred millions of these exquisite heavenly nymphs sprang
 forth.
 And the servant girls whom they had with them were innumerable.

35 But neither the gods nor the demons accepted them [as wives].
 Since they were not accepted they came to be known as belonging to all.

36 Then Vāruṇī the illustrious daughter of Varuṇa emerged.
 She was seeking acceptance.

37 The sons of Diti did not receive that daughter of Varuṇa.
 But the sons of Aditi did receive that blameless maiden.

38 Therefore the sons of Diti are demons (*asuras*)
 And the sons of Aditi gods (*suras*)[7]—
 And the gods were overjoyed because they had received Vāruṇī.

39 The noble king of horses, Uccaiḥśravas, came from the ocean
 too.
 Likewise Kaustubha, that most precious jewel [ornament of
 Viṣṇu].
 And also the supreme juice Immortality.

---

7. Vāruṇī is related to *sura*, wine or intoxicating beverages in general. The
fanciful etymology explains the demons (who did not accept her) as *a-suras*, and
the gods (who did accept her) as *suras*. Thus the commentary *Tilaka* by Rama interprets the text. However, see supra, p. 75.

40 Then because of this juice the fall of the house was cata-
   strophic.
   The sons of Aditi fought Diti's sons.

41 Together with the ogres all demons united
   And the fight was terrifying
   And overwhelmed the whole threefold world.

42 When all had been destroyed,
   The powerful Viṣṇu took on his form of deluding magic
   And quickly took away the juice Immortality.

43 Those who turned to Viṣṇu, the imperishable, the supreme
   Puruṣa,
   Were destroyed in the fight by Viṣṇu the Lord.

44 After the defeat of the demons,
   Indra, the king of gods, ascended the throne and happily began
   his dominion
   Over the worlds with their seers and angelic singers.

8 ✿
A
Final
Examination

W E S H O U L D admit that the "humor" of myth turned out to be quite serious, not just in some, but in most instances. Still, there is no reason to drop the word. It is undeniable that most myths resist the solemnity of a purely philosophical explanation and, above all, that most myths do not allow for a profound, exclusively mystical interpretation.

The literary category of "humor" is not a substitute for philosophical reasonings or mystical awareness. But it may be a welcome addition. In many cases it prevents excesses in interpretive zeal. It protects us from the heavy-handedness to which the best serious intentions too often lead.

A certain heavy-handedness exists in the treatment of myth by Malinowski; we suggested before that his characterization of myth as a "hard-working, extremely important cultural force" is not quite as easily applicable as it seems to be.[1] Myth gives a concrete form to man's freedom, it is a form moreover which is not provided by any other means. As we have seen, the cosmogonic myth can sometimes function in the face of death. But such seriousness, even the seriousness of death, should not blind us to the "playful" character of myth. The point is that the myth does indeed *function*, and in that respect it differs considerably from what we in our "academized" world consider serious. It is certain that the Ngaju Dayak who is confronted with death does not sit down and systematize his gloom, not even in terms of a serious existential philosophy. The point is simple and yet may need some elaboration, for there is a real danger that we might view the cosmogony with too great a solemnity, with a misplaced seriousness.

We have seen the efficacy of myth: the myth is not a theory. It is first and foremost something that happens; it is *recited, chanted, enacted.* But who are we to register these facts in our theoretical considerations? Our lives are governed by fashions that seem least amenable to such happenings. We, the people who rehearse for weddings. We, who are told at academic processions by a special dignitary on which side (to the right or the left of the forehead) to dangle the tassel. We have substituted external solemnity for the sort of event that is presented in the cosmogonic myth. We have substituted ceremony for liturgy. This type of substitution hampers our understanding of myth.

We should realize, however, that this is not all that can be

1. *Supra*, p. 50.

said. Our obsession to act in conformity with a preconceived theory is only a rather recent phenomenon. It is no doubt immediately tied up with our modern zeal for general education. The more schooling, the more preoccupation with general, theoretical notions. But this should not of course lead us to believe that the whole world consists only of materials for our theoretical reflexion. Quite obviously, religious man in all times and places demands more than such treatment.

In dealing with the cosmogonic event, we should remember that our preoccupation with theories in no way determines our whole being. We cannot appeal to the habits of our "academized" world to create the illusion that there is still an unbridgeable gulf between the realms in which cosmogonic myths function and ourselves.

First of all, we too know moments of true liturgy. This is particularly clear when tragedy strikes. It was not only because of the greatness of the event that the burial of President Kennedy was not "just a ceremony." Rather, it was true liturgy because its meaning obviously did not depend on the accurate rehearsal of each participant in each detail. No one could have regulated the mourning by so many on that day. Conflicting and piecemeal theories became irrelevant; spontaneously, people subjected themselves to an order which appeared to govern both life and death.

Such moments are moments of true liturgy, which is indeed the most serious "play" that we can experience. Although the things done and said on those occasions may have been done and said a thousand times before, we are participants, even if we watch at a distance. Strange as it may seem, such moments grant a peculiar strength and determination. With Malinowski's word we might think of a "cultural force." All nations recount their history by pointing to critical events and derive their power from them. Such events have a mythical function. Paradoxically—and in that respect like so many myths—strength and unity of a people are felt to be born in adversity. The designation "cultural force" may still smack somewhat of the external observer's jargon. If we attempt to understand myth, and if we realize our own sources of strength (recounting the history of our origin), or the rare events of true liturgical experience, it might be more accurate to say, myth restores the freedom to live in the world as it is. Granted that myth is a cultural force with all its observable purposefulness, it is above all the specific form which leads to renewal for life. This positive freedom, the liberation for the sake of life, is attained by the myth's power to liberate man from the exhausting and deadening order of things in his common experience.

Here in particular it makes sense to speak of playfulness and to speak of humorous aspects without apology. With some reservation we might still accept Malinowski's characterization of myth as "an extremely important cultural force," but the adjective "hard-working" seems out of place in most instances. It suggests the backdrop of the poor savage, having a hard time making ends meet, and sorely in need of an ideological lift. Such a suggestion is far too academic. One could hardly characterize the creation myth of the Ngaju Dayak recited in the funeral as "hard-working." The myth which tells us of a previous world made of lac inhabited by people with a liquor still,[2] and the grotesque generally, defy the word "hard-working." The Churning of the Ocean, the myth transmitted by the Indian Epics, with all its fantastic traits has a great

2. *Supra*, p. 67.

deal to say about hard work, but one would hesitate to qualify the myth itself as hard-working.

It is obvious that myth is essential to the human constitution. The liberation granted through it is fundamental to man's existence. This fact itself makes the endeavor to define myth in terms of one function or aspect of man futile, no matter how academically established the study of this one function or aspect is. Myth does not argue; it always addresses itself to man about man's total world. Consequently, myth bears on philosophy, psychology, sociology, cultural anthropology, and many another academic specialization. But none of these specializations can deal with myth exhaustively. We have seen before the restrictions of dealing with myth through philosophical analysis or even by presupposing mystical experiences.

We have made an attempt to find out what could be said about the structure of myth without binding ourselves to one function or aspect. Our discussion of Malinowski's general statement about myth served as a reminder of the necessity to go beyond specialization. We did not expect to arrive at a new definition with all the limitations implied by such an attempt. Aware of the fascination of myth, we tried to indicate what presented itself as most obvious: the "looseness" and the "humorous aspect" which escape definition by specialists. Let us summarize our findings.

First of all, myth renews man's existence by breaking through the extreme oppositions under whose sway his life is lived: the opposites of the highest and the lowest, the most creative and the most destructive, life and death, good and evil, day and night, and so on. It is exactly in the "impossible possibility" of this breakthrough, in contrast to all our experience, that the freedom or renewal of man's possibilities is effected. It is this first moment, the "dimming of the opposites," which shows the strongest mystical signs.

Secondly, the real point of myth becomes accessible in a flash, from an unexpected angle, and contrary to orderly arrangements of facts. ("The inverse effect.")

Thirdly, there is an awareness of the mystery which makes the sacred available. The myth speaks through presentation, not by argumentation; and its peculiar authority stands out more clearly through the awareness of subjective witness or transmission ("subjective reservedness").

Fourthly, there is the "grotesque." Just like the first type or moment breaks through the great opposites, the "grotesque" breaks through the humdrum of accepted experiences, measures, and reasonings.

In all four moments, myth destroys the oppressive finiteness of man. The cosmogonic myth is indeed fundamental, for it can be said to disrupt the "profanity" of existence in a paradigmatic way. The cosmogony presents the basis of life in recounting the origin of the world. Simultaneously, it renews the freedom of man. Because of the recognition of this simultaneity we have come further in our understanding of myth than the older generation: we now know that we are not speaking of stages in the development of mankind when we broach the subject of myth. The form of freedom, the orientation which is presented in myth, is not available through any of our specializations. Myth, especially the cosmogonic myth, is the basis of human life, and, regardless of its first occurrence, it has come to stay.

It is not by coincidence that our considerations of myth have led us several times to modern poetry. Imagery and experience called forth by poets are intrinsically related to cosmogonic imagery. Indeed,

the past does not exist for the true poet; the poet discovers the world as if he were present at the world's origin, as if he were contemporary with the first day of Creation. One might say that every great poet re-fashions the world, for he attempts to look at it as if time and history did not exist.[3]

The poet does not seem to be bound by any traditional form or criterion. He does with language what is ordinarily not done. Of course, this does not make all poetry by definition mythical. But the closest kinship exists in the endeavor to re-create the world, the abandonment of ordinary time and speech, and, above all, in the attempt to bring about a certain liberation from set patterns of thought. The poet is able to recognize most keenly the danger of disastrous set patterns:

> *This structure of ideas, these ghostly sequences*
> *Of the mind, result only in disaster . . .*[4]

The scholarly temptation is to define and to search exclusively for causal connections, and, by following the "ghostly sequences of the mind," chain anew with the help of ideas. It is a temptation which myth does not foster.

Myth is, among other things, poetic literature which aims at freedom from mere ideas. It is and does even more than that, as we have seen. Myth does at least one thing which admittedly very

3. M. Eliade, "Les mythes du monde moderne," *Mythes, rêves et mystères* (Paris: Gallimard, 1957), pp. 33–34.
4. Wallace Stevens, *The Collected Poems*, p. 326.

little modern poetry does: it speaks with authority and determination.

The word of myth is decisive. How does it decide something? By giving it a form. The word of myth does not kill like the concept which abstracts from life, but it calls forth life; no sharper contrast with mere theory is conceivable.[5]

Although few poets can be said to speak with such creative decisiveness at present, those who do speak show that the urge for cosmogonic imagery is not only a thing of the past. It is especially in the refusal to accept common experience as ultimately valid that the inner kinship shows up.

From the perspective of good poetry as well as of myth (if we are allowed to *argue* from that perspective for a moment), the trouble with the world of man is exactly that things are supposed to and expected to lead somewhere all of the time: it is the "woodenness" of the common experience and inference. This "woodenness" is broken, high and low, unexpectedly and mysteriously, by the new forms that are created.

We are trying to be faithful to our decision not to fall a victim to a fixation on one single aspect of myth. But we realize that this effort brings us inevitably to the limits of what is academically possible.

There is a close relation between the specificity of the mythical creation and the mysterious specificity of man, better known, but not explained as, his "uniqueness." Academically, it is quite possible and common practice to speak about "cultural forces," because, for all their mysteriousness, they seem more tangible than

5. G. van der Leeuw, *La religion dans son essence et ses manifestations* (Paris: Payot, 1948), p. 405 (sec. 60, 1).

the mystery of man. In regard to cosmogonic myth, it has been common opinion that its major function is the maintenance of the status quo, or the preservation of the permanence of life.

It should be confessed that our whole essay is somewhat at variance with these accepted possibilities and respectable procedures of explanation, although we have stressed time and again that we did not want to offer other interpretations instead of the existing ones. We are still unwilling to venture a definition, but we should say that we are unwilling to do so because of the character of myth itself. Speaking about the creation myth's tendency to preserve and maintain life is ascribing a tendency to myth which, as a rule, is not borne out by the text. To speak of the maintenance of the status quo is certainly to impute something to the myth. The abstract categories of preservation (of life) and of a status quo (in society and politics) are categories with a character external to the myth's structure; they are coined in the disciplines observing reality which are, from the point of view of myth, profane. The learned labels evoke the image of a student patting the poet of myth on the back and telling him that his doings are useful indeed for the community. It is as if a justice of the Supreme Court were to go from campus to campus making speeches about the usefulness of religion courses in our colleges, telling his audience that religion is a good thing for the life of the nation and that we cannot have enough of it. Somehow, the real point seems lost, in spite of the fact that reasonings and labels seem immaculate and presented with authority.

We could not very well speak of a status quo in terms of the contents of a cosmogonic myth. In most instances, however, we could notice its strict form. But stylization and subsequent memorization in this stylized form are inevitable. Stylization is an easily observable feature in modern poetry also. When classical models are given up, and when consciously the most vernacular of vernaculars is used, the *saying* will still be different from "profane," everyday speech.

One step closer to the real problem at stake behind discussions concerning a supposed interest of the myth in the status quo is the fact that no myth remains unchanged for ever. Even more than that: myths are lost altogether and replaced by others. In most cases a relationship between myth and culture is evident; hunters do not tell the same myth that is current in urban, agricultural societies. But does that mean that the new myth is merely a reflection of changed socioeconomic conditionings? By no means. There are just too many individual differences. This brings us back again to the specificity of man and myth. Myths change and are replaced. There is no single factor or set of factors that explains these things.

If here too we do not want to enforce the preoccupation with one aspect of life on the whole problem of man and myth, we should simply state as a fact that every mythology can turn stale and ask for renewal, or even for the eruption of a new one. Such eruption may or may not relate to socioeconomic conditions, but at any rate it will be in perfect harmony with what we have observed in the structure of myth in terms of man's "cosmogonic propensity." There will be the impossibility of man to live permanently with the deadening commonness of his experiences and accepted measures. The old myth may have become part of the commonness and, if no addition or repair is possible, give way to a new one. Man's freedom has to be re-established. In any event, the new myth will bring the opposites together, the inverse effect will be there, it will be profusely grotesque; at the same time, its conveyance will be mysterious, as if it were not new. And indeed it could not be, for it will tell of *illud tempus* and tell man with authority all things necessary to know in immeasurable measures. The final question which was first, man or this new myth, is not really a final question. It can be raised only by the heretically superficial academician in ourselves, who insists on the irrelevant aspect rather than lose himself in the uniqueness of man.

Part **II** MYTH AND MYSTICISM

9 ❦
Reconnaissance

ISCUSSING MYTH, we have not refrained from quoting
some texts that are known from mystical literature.
In explaining the "inverse effect" we quoted a passage
by the famous mystic Jakob Boehme (pp. 51–52). A text
from another mystical tradition, the Kabbalah, served
us to illustrate the "dimming of the opposites" (p. 46).
Without going into the problem, we mentioned in passing
the mystical quality of the famous Ṛgvedic creation
hymn (p. 44). I do not think anyone would object to
these references, for they illustrated the peculiarity of
mythical expressions quite well. Nevertheless, the question
cannot very well be omitted: what is the relationship

between myth and mysticism? The subject is complex, and it seems to me that some lengthy reasonings are inevitable.

Broaching the subject of mysticism requires caution. Next to the complex problem of how mysticism relates to myth, we have the equally important and equally complex problem of their distinctiveness. There are several ways in which we can distort the discussion unintentionally. It will be best to make this clear.

There is no generally accepted, authoritative understanding of what mysticism is, in spite of the fact that there is general agreement when we refer to a number of people in various religious traditions as mystics. Without hesitancy, historians point to the mysticism of certain individuals: a Plotinus, Ruusbroec, Eckhart, Nicholas of Cusa, Kapila, Śaṃkara, Nāgārjuna, in all parts of the world and in all periods. A few of those mystics can even be said to have "made school." Hence we hear also of mystical traditions and movements, as Sufism in the Islamic world; and the rise of monasticism and spiritual orders in the Christian world would be unthinkable without such mystics as Augustine, Francis of Assisi, or Ignatius of Loyola.

This common agreement in which we all follow what scholars and books tell us should not make us forget that we are lacking a standard definition of mysticism. In the case of mystical documents, much more so than with the subject of myth, we are looking at matters far superior to ourselves and to our ordinary level of comprehension. It may be unpleasant to say this at a moment when we are proud of the extent to which we have democratized our education, but to ignore the hierarchy built into the religious documents of man would be misleading. Mystic writings bespeak exceptionally great authors, and that may well be the major reason why we are at a loss in our attempts at definitions. And even if we should refuse to accept that inroad on our intellectual self-esteem, the scholarly arguments taking place on our own level of discourse would soon subdue us. The fact is that scholarly investigations have failed to come up with an unequivocal definition of mysticism.

Someone might interject here, why is it that "scholars" should understand "mystics?" The question is not as facetious as it may seem, and a serious reply may be given. Somewhat in anticipation of further discussion, the answer would be: Scholars have an immediate access to our view of life and influence it to quite an extent. Therefore, what they say about mystics who are significant figures in so many religious traditions is important, also when they disagree among themselves, and should concern us.

For some it is a matter of incommunicable feeling granted to gifted individuals, for others a matter of disciplined experience that at least to some extent can be taught; as to its trustworthiness, one sees its basis in the will, another stresses intuition, a third one the rational coherence of the mystical experience, a fourth one insists on a type of cognition all by itself, untranslatable into another type of sensing or reasoning; as to the goal of the mystic's path, attempts at definition lead into a jungle of puzzles: is it an absorption into the godhead, an identification of the mystic with God, is it an emancipation of the individual beyond the bonds of the world (and without any notion of God), is it an identity of the experiencer with the universe? Any choice from these and more possibilities can be used to forge a definition, and a number of mystical texts can be adduced as evidence in each case.[1] Specific texts and general statements about mysticism seem to exclude each

1. A very illuminating discussion on this scholarly diversity is given by Richard H. Robinson, *Early Mādhyamika in India and China* (Madison: University of Wisconsin Press, 1967), Chapter I: "Questions and Method."

other. Statements about mysticism fall short of defining it. Indeed, if "mysticism" has any unity at all and if the word is useful in describing so many different things, the only sensible conclusion is that our ordinary use of speech does not suffice to define the many phenomena of mysticism exhaustively.

Is not this problem analogous to the problem we faced in delineating myth? I think so, but certainly the problem is intensified in the case of mysticism. Looking at mystical texts, most of us, most of the time, are like tribal people, technically ignorant, looking at airplanes, knowing about them only by seeing them in their flight. Myth and mysticism are by no means unrelated, but when we reflect on what we can *say* about the two, the differences are striking.

Mysticism is certainly, among other things, a matter of religious *experience*. Our problem in speaking about it is compounded by the fact that recent scholarship dealing with religion is not preoccupied with experience, but rather with empirical observation, with forms that appear ("phenomena"). Studying given forms (cultic acts, symbolisms, and so on) makes it possible to avoid undue speculation on the "ultimate truth" of religious convictions. It also makes it possible to avoid uncertain and unverifiable statements about the inner feelings of individuals. But since mysticism is inseparable from experience, this modern concern for soundness may be a mixed blessing for our present discussion.

In the preceding pages we too have spoken of given religious *forms*, namely, the creation myths. We have seen analogies to forms in our own modern life that have shown that the ancient and distant stories are not alien to us. We could even conclude that human life *in general* depends on mythical expression. There is an objective quality about our findings in the study of myth because mythical *forms* (of whatever great variety) are inevitable *forms* of all human life.

Our situation with respect to mysticism is indeed different. Not only does it bring in the element of experience which is always hard to assess, but at the same time it presents us with the problem of individuality which is much more difficult to discuss than the general features of human life given with the religious expression and literatures of all nations. In short, all people are religious, whether they know it or not, but not all people are mystics, even though in some religious traditions mystics have coined forms of religious expression that became generally accepted.

It is necessary to reflect on this in order to realize the nature and limits of our understanding of a relation between myth and mysticism.

Our findings with respect to myth have shown that there is no reason for assuming that myths as such owe their making to a special age, dubbed "mythopoeic" or "primitive." All ages have their mythopoets. For all men, if they are men at all, give a form to their freedom, which is always more than a matter of economic necessities and goals or of social or individual wants. Of course, this supreme freedom documented in myths is not always the same, although it is precisely because of this supremacy that we can recognize myths in traditions different from our own, for we know ourselves of a comparable thirst for supremacy. Myths vary from one time to the next and from place to place. A myth recorded in the Rāmāyaṇa differs greatly from a myth of some island in the Pacific, and both differ equally from the poetic gropings for a supreme freedom in Wallace Stevens's work. Does this mean that we are merely pushing the problem of myth and its formation from one obscure corner to another equally obscure, now that we have given up the idea of a specific age in the history of mankind capable of creating myths? No, for the setting is now totally different from any evolutionistic view. The great objection to be leveled against all talk about a mythopoeic age is exactly this—that it is based on untenable evolutionistic ideas. Our view of myth is based on the sound historical realization that no period is ever the same as another, while all produce myths. In different ages, different relations exist, for example, between poets, priests and scholars. Different ideologies determine their place and function.

All this is so obvious that it seems trite to underscore it. Yet the mistakes made in the reading of myths are so elementary that even the obvious must be said at times. More seriously still, the obstacles created in the reading of myths are often so artificial and unnecessary, that the obvious may serve a very practical purpose.

It is not for the first time that we owe the clearest expression of a crucial and elementary insight not to a historian of religion but to a philosopher. The philosopher Alphonse de Waelhens has demonstrated more cogently than anyone I know a point we should be fully conscious of in speaking of myth: We are never in a position to see the features of a myth clearly, to objectify a myth as myth, *until we have somehow overcome it.*[2] Indeed, it is possible for us today to speak of the nineteenth-century "myth of scientific optimism," or of the eighteenth-century "myth of man's well-nigh perfected reason." In so doing, we are certain that we

2. Alphonse de Waelhens, "Le mythe de la démythification," in Enrico Castelli (ed.), *Mythe et Foi*, Actes du colloque organisé par le centre international d'études humanistes et par l'institut d'études philosophiques de Rome, Rome, 6–12 janvier 1966 (Paris: Aubier, 1966), pp. 251–261.

identify rather neatly myths around which a whole era or a whole culture revolved or recognized itself at its climactic points.

In each case, we can delineate the myth only because for us it no longer functions as myth. The distance between it and ourselves enables us to see its outline. "Overcoming" a myth thus implies a "leaving behind." At the same time this or that myth of the past is among the materials we need to orient ourselves. Therefore, "overcoming" a myth implies also a definite incorporation into our own view of history and the view of our place in it.

"Overcoming" the myth then should not be understood as "destroying" or "rejecting." Whether we like or dislike the eighteenth-century enthusiasm for reason or the nineteenth-century scientific optimism, we still have to determine the proper place of reason and science at our turn. In each case, we who are speaking here and now must first draw a wider circle in which we think we can assign the proper place to each myth.

The case of the myths of distant and ancient peoples is not too different from the myths of cultural periods so near to us as the eigtheenth or nineteenth century. No people whose myths we study has ever said or left a clear message saying, Look, here you have our myths which we *en masse* hold to be true. Critical scholars have taught us that the famous creation account of Genesis 1 is an appendix that was prefixed to an already complex bundle of religious writings. The myths we have before us from various primitive communities in neat printed translations are never the sum of their creed but more often a fraction of a complicated tradition, a fraction in volume and time, selected only in the best of cases by local discrimination and sensitivity.

How could it be otherwise? The situation is given with the

living and changing tradition we study and with the living and changing means and abilities for understanding that we bring to bear on it. Even when we call a civilization "closed" or "dead" —as in the case of ancient Egypt—our own means and abilities for understanding continue to change. The latter are part of *our myth*—wider, more embracing than the myths we interpret; in fact, so wide is this myth of ours that within it we designate or intend to designate the place of all myths. It seems a remarkable and very conceited undertaking. We set great store by it and believe in its soundness when we want to say something about man's myths. And is it really so conceited, or are we only performing the function that mythology has always enabled man to perform? It would have been conceited to stand aside and look from a safe and secure place at both narration and interpretation of myths, with the help of some objective and eternal category. But if for a moment we might have thought the category of "humor," borrowed from literary essayists and for that reason truly an external tool, would grant us such safe outside stance, we realize at once that even this closest approximation of an objective instrument is insecure. "Humor" has not been more for us than a collective term for a bundle of diverse features proper to all mythological literature. Moreover, the notion of "humor" as a tool of conscious understanding is barely a century and a half old. It is part of the language we live with; we must use it for it serves us best; it is part of our mythology.

In reality we cannot stand aside. On whatever level it happens, our interpreting of myth is our own mythological activity, an activity we engage in *qua* human beings, conceited ones and humble ones alike. Like all writing of history, our interpretation of myths has its day and will pass. Yesterday's myths are "mere myths" today. The myth of today will be "mere myth" tomorrow.

The activity of interpreting myths becomes dizzying, but our reflexions will serve us in the end to get a better view of mysticism and its importance for myth. The sensation of vertigo is inevitable in the undertaking. For let us realize the meaning of the interpretation of myths. It is good and well to say that it is among the highest activities of man; not only does it literally involve our doings to our neighbor, but it is immediately connected with the profoundest and last statements we can make about our own existence. But it also means to be engulfed in a play of ever widening waves, and from where we are it is not possible to say where the waves began and where they end. I think of a most suggestive picture on a tin of cocoa—a picture of a nurse who holds in her hand an identical cocoa can, while the nurse on the can she holds is holding another can, ad infinitum. One thinks, holding that tin, where is the end? And especially, who is holding me?

In view of the subject of myth, a picture of such limitless involution and evolution may seem to lead to a hopeless relativism and futility. But that conclusion is not necessary—apart from the fact that it might be called a hasty mythologism. On one hand, we know from all the myths we have looked at that a sense of futility did not have to wait for our scholarship-ridden world to arise and that man in his most valued myths can show himself perfectly aware of the endlessness of his universe and his doings therein. On the other hand, we too, in the activity of establishing the place of myths, cannot utter words like "relativism" and "endlessness" without immediately qualifying these terms. It must be said that each new mythological syndrome, no matter how relative it is, is nevertheless capable of embracing all preceding ones; for that reason every new myth is indeed new.[3] Hence the discouraging and typical overtone of "relativism," to wit, *repetitiousness*, fades. And as to endlessness, we must concede that this very notion must be caught in a picture: our image of man in a valuable endeavor to understand himself. "Endlessness" evokes an image that seems well suited for the travels through history in which we try to come to terms with myth.

When we reflect on our intellectual travels through history as endless, we still submit ourselves to only one major image. To be sure, traveling may be the wayfaring of a pilgrim or of a salesman, but "being on the move" certainly seems a standard image of our culture, literally and figuratively. We have even elevated the image to a science: cybernetics, the complex mathematical science of piloting our way into problems that we cannot identify through traditional calculations. The idea of never quite getting there or arriving at new problems that require new scientific efforts is perhaps not even frightening. We recognize it as the way of all our sciences. Next to this picture of endlessness, no matter how complex, there are many more.

Hunter tribes like those of Northern Siberia have always been in need of traveling. Their livelihood depended directly on the reindeer and other game. The necessity of roaming the earth colored their myths and all their literature profoundly.[4] It is evident however that their wanderings for so many centuries were much more immediate and down-to-earth than the wanderings that led to cybernetics. In other words, it is possible to conceive

3. This point too has been well made by A. de Waelhens, *op. cit.*

4. See William W. Malandra, "The Concept of Movement in History of Religions: a Religio-Historical Study of Reindeer in the Spiritual Life of North Eurasian Peoples," *Numen* XIV (1967), 23–69.

of a world where endlessness would be at home and not be experienced in conjunction with the kind of relativism that made us sigh.

Or again, it is possible to think of endlessness in terms of an ancient Indian tradition. The waters on the earth evaporate under the heat of the sun and return again as rain, they evaporate again and return unceasingly. This is not mere allegory, it expresses a precise image of man's world, the world as *saṃsāra*, the endless flowing of existence. Within this universal and eternal course the finiteness of a man's life and work seems to make him insignificant. Yet, this endlessness, *saṃsāra*, reveals its nature precisely in the realization that it consists in the succession of such finitenesses and exists in the heart of the finite.

Just like a caterpillar when it comes to the end of a blade of grass, beginning to move toward the next one, draws itself together for the move, so does man's self, leaving the body and giving up his wonted ignorance, draw itself together for another move.[5]

According to Indian tradition, knowledge begins in gaining this sight of this endlessness. The process of gaining true knowledge is the real task of man. Its endlessness is very different from the tribal nomadic wanderings, and also from the imagery of our modern scientific pursuits. It is a process of unveiling rather than traveling. The final moment of the unveiling, of entering depth rather than distance, is never immediately visible, but its certainty is not doubted.

Another Indian tradition depicts endlessness in a manner that seems to complete the previous one. Still it has a distinction

5. Bṛhadāraṇyaka Upaniṣad 4, 4, 3.

of its own and has become prominent in Buddhism especially. It connects the two endless processes: that of the all-devouring circle of existence and that of gaining supreme wisdom. For proper understanding of the endless impermanence of the world is identical with the power to annihilate the cause of impermanence. A double movement is inspired by the waterwheel, its pictorial expression. Well known in the culture of wet ricefields, it scoops the water up in a perennial movement and empties itself without ever changing. One of the great titles of the Buddha himself is *cakravartin*, that is, at the same time, "the propeller of the wheel" (the wheel of liberation from bondage to the world), and "universal emperor." The endless evolvement of the world contains its own reversal in the enlightenment of the wise.[6] A new, clear mythology is born, focusing on man's problems with endlessness.

It will not be necessary to multiply examples of mythologies of endlessness. The few lines drawn here make clear that our own thoughts about the endlessness of our investigations of myth do not only arise from the myths we study but are part of a mythology of which we can only be dimly aware.

But besides endlessness, the pursuit of myths gives one a more painful sensation. It is the limitation and unoriginality of our own profoundest thoughts and feelings. For the fact that we find ourselves guided by a certain imagery in the endlessness of our task is significant. We did not create that imagery. On the contrary, it almost seems to create us. Our earlier observation that all people may be called religious but not all may be called mystics will here be examined on its consequences.

All of us have experiences that make a profound impression

6. See the magnificent study by Paul Mus, *La notion de temps réversible dans la mythologie bouddhique* (Melun: Imprimerie Administrative, 1939).

on us, whether painful or pleasant. We may express them, but we hardly ever govern the channels through which they are expressed. André Gide observed that soldiers coming back from the front in the first World War spoke of their feelings by means of the clichés from the language of journalists who themselves had had no experience of war.[7] The example is poignant, yet in tune with everyday events we know of without much further meditation. Precisely those experiences that strike us most and render us "at a loss for words" cause us to fall back on *models* of expression that are or have become generally accepted.

This fact, recognized without difficulty by a simple psychology, is confirmed a hundredfold in the area of myth. After all, myths always deal with the most crucial, the most "existential" problems and mysteries of life. No nation has ever consisted of sharp-witted philosophers who gave all their time and energy to those ultimate questions. This is the other side of the thesis that myths are understandable for us all. We understand them because we all know from our experience about similar authoritative models that provide us with expressions where our individual creativeness fails. Without them we would be reduced to a subhuman level of experience. *They give us the freedom of human expression.* We do not understand them to the extent that we can create new myths at will.

In an age in which the praises of individualism are sung, these reflexions cannot be entirely welcome. For they contain a criticism of a type of existential philosophy that is generally and implicitly accepted. It simply is not true that crisis situations, in great suffering or despair, per se change man, lead him to profound

7. Jean Starobinski, "The Idea of Nostalgia," *Diogenes* 54 (Summer, 1966), p. 82.

insights or enable him to make the "leap of faith." If that were so, the survivors of concentration camps, of the Korean or Vietnamese wars would all be very different from most of their neighbors. Now and ever, profound and revolutionary changes in man's consciousness, in his experience and expression, deviating from the dominant mythology, are the exception and not the rule.

In every community and tradition exceptions occur. These are the great revolutionaries in the history of man's mythology, who do not just reform but forcefully attack the common underlying certainties of the society. They create new openings in a closed world of thought and sometimes have to bear the consequences of their impiety. It can hardly be otherwise, now as in the past, no matter how much the prophet may proclaim the real intentions of the accepted traditions. The line between revolution and reformation, between prophet and rebel has often been hard to discern.

Among the exceptions are the mystics. They are hardly ever violent, not always forceful, many of them women. Yet, as in the case of the prophets, we see certain "deviations" from the public opinion about sacred traditions. Their activities may not be rebellious; more often than not they may be faithful readers of the authoritative religious scriptures, but their experience and understanding is not that of the crowd. They may be consciously in tune with the general religious tradition, but in many cases their mysticism can equally be regarded as secular. Certainly, if we speak of them as a distinct group because of their unique position vis-à-vis the ruling mythical ideas, we must say that they have made the most lasting expressions. Of all myth-makers, they have perhaps contributed most to the formulation of new myths. Why would their expressions have been of such lasting endurance? Our discussion so far has already hinted at the answer. The mystics' willingness to struggle with the final questions of whatever tradition or human situation and their ability and power to test them by their experience has always meant looking through the contingencies of any given myth. Hence the sort of endlessness of which we have merely caught a glimpse in our problem of interpreting myths is seen by them in its own nature, most perfectly and most generally and therefore least dependent on the coincidences of history. Their expression, even if caught only in part, has never failed to provide sustenance and comfort to others, less gifted than they. As we shall see, the validity of mystical formulations cannot be disputed any more than the statements of a myth can be argued. Perhaps very few mystics have ever composed myths, but the indisputable validity of their experiences and expressions made insertion in myth natural as soon as a mystic's experience was felt as authoritative in a human community.

10 ❦
Subjectivity and Objectivity

H ow can we speak of mysticism if it is so distinct from everything we normally agree on and from the very myths underlying our agreements? How can we make sense in studying it if it goes against the grain of our common understanding? Above all, how can we speak of mysticism meaningfully if specific *individual* experiences are essential to it?

Our reflections so far should make us cautious and averse to hasty conclusions. It will not be advisable or necessary to commit the sort of error that at one time became fashionable in New Testament scholarship: establishing the impossibility of writing a "life of Jesus" and proceeding

112

to write one. Mysticism may be undefinable; mystics may be very different from us commoners; inaccessible they are not. Those we can speak about left us documents: they wanted to communicate; they themselves felt that their experiences related to matters of general import. Certainly it will be possible to understand something of the connection between mysticism and myth that we mentioned and had occasion to refer to briefly before (pp. 110–111). It will be to the point, however, to begin by clearing up some common misunderstandings surrounding any discussion of religious experience in general and mystical experience in particular.

It is to the point to emphasize that the experience of the mystic must not be confused with mere personal *emotions*. The documents rather insist on a more objective quality. More than "mere" experience, the mystic experience is knowledge.

To think of certain experiences with such a positive evaluation is not strange from the point of view of generally accessible religious traditions. Very well known is the biblical language in which the same verb can be translated as "to know" and "to have sexual intercourse": Adam *knew* Eve. It is very clear in such cases that the realm of the senses and the realm of the mind do not have to be kept as separate as we normally think we are keeping them. *Jñāna*, the Sanskrit word most often translated as "knowledge" is not just "a body of information," but connotes at the same time the *process* of knowing, particularly that process that assures the thinker's freedom from worldly bondage. It implies experience, and, *vice versa*, every true experience leads to "knowledge." With examples such as these in mind it is certainly not possible to explain mystic experience, but it will make it easier to see that we do not have to create additional oppositions between it and existing traditions.

More significantly, authoritative religious spokesmen who were well aware of the singular importance of mysticism have not hesitated to stress the knowledge element of the mystic experience. In Western tradition, according to Thomas Aquinas in his *Summa Theologiae*, mysticism is the *cognitio Dei experimentalis*, the knowledge of God by experiment (or by way of experience). The mystical theologian Jean Gerson gave this definition: "Theologia mystica est experimentalis cognitio habita de Deo per amoris unitivi complexum." (Mystical theology is knowledge of God by experience, arrived at through the embrace of unifying love.)[1] Christian theological tradition distinguishes "mystical theology" from "natural theology" and "dogmatic theology."[2] The first is established by means of experience, the second by reason, the third by revelation. Thus a legitimate place is provided for the mystical experience, side by side with the other types of theology. The validity of its knowledge is accepted in principle.

The subject of "experience" raises a problem among us, especially when qualified with the adjective "individual." I have in mind that in wide circles, almost unconsciously, religious matters in general are associated with individual feelings which as such are thought to be concealed from other people. Not only is this a recent habit of thought—stimulated in America even in the most intellectual milieus by protestant pietistic sectarianism—but it does not apply to the vast majority of religious phenomena. Needless to add, our previous chapters about myth should not really allow our present discussion to be obscured by this rather superficial association. The fact that with mysticism we have to speak of ex-

1. T. Corbishley's article on Mysticism in the *New Catholic Encyclopedia* (New York: McGraw-Hill, 1967), X, 175.
2. *Ibid.*

perience, however, inevitably raises the question of individual—and hence, it would seem, really unapproachable—emotions with new force.

In conjunction with other theoretical notions, the association of religion with individual experience has also had its heyday in scholarship in our century. Accordingly, mysticism has often been regarded as the area in which "true" religion was manifest. Perhaps it is not wrong to see in mysticism the highest possible religious expressions, but much depends on the manner in which such a thesis is put forward.

An astounding influence on the study of religion came from Rudolf Otto. In his most widely read work, *Das Heilige* (first edition 1917), but also in other works, mysticism is a central theme. It is especially in mystical experiences that man has access to the holy. This is not the place to discuss the nuances and the great erudition in Otto's work which fully account for the impression his ideas made on specialistic philologists, historians, philosophers, and theologians. His theory of "the holy" as "the absolutely other," as such irreducible to rational or ethical terms, has come under attack, particularly in the last few years.[3] Otto has become suspect of concealing with his theory on religious experience an apology for the Christian faith, for it is always in the Christian

3. Sharp criticism has been leveled against Otto and his influence from a more or less Marxistic angle: Kurt Rudolph, "Die Problematik der Religionswissenschaft als akademisches Lehrfach," *Kairos* IX, 1 (1967), 22–42 (See also the bibliography there given); Vittorio Lanternari, *La grande festa* (Milano: Il Saggiatore, 1959), Chap. I. However, criticism has not been lacking earlier and in other circles: Renato Boccasino, "La religione dei primitive," in P. Tacchi Venturi (ed.), *Storia delle religioni* (first published 1934; 4th ed. Torino: Unione Tipografico, 1954), p. 106. Still earlier: W. Schmidt, S.V.D., *Menschheitswege zum Gotterkennen: rationale, irrationale, superrationale* (Monaco, 1923).

realm, more especially Luther, that the purest experiences are found by him. The suspicion is confirmed by the manner in which he unfolds his evolutionistic views on the religious history of mankind. He theorizes on the experiences of early humanity which could only appear as "crude." It is by slow degrees that the "numinous" is revealed in human consciousness through the ages. ("Numinous" is Otto's term for the holy in isolation: without our modern overtones of morality and rationality.)

Today few serious scholars would accept Otto's implications of a general evolution of man's religious experience. It is here that we should remember that the notion of evolution owes its strength to such sciences as biology and geology, counting in many tens and hundreds of thousands of years. Compared with such stretches of time, the couple of millennia for which we have mystical writings (with critical annotations, and so on) are too short a period on which to apply the term "evolution" meaningfully. Above all, the assumption that the writings of Śaṃkara, Eckhart, or a Zen master can be seen as indicative of the ascending line of human religious consciousness seems absurd. In spite of his truly important work— surpassing this "experiential evolutionism" by far—Otto has been widely quoted as if he were no more than the spokesman for an evolutionistically oriented scholarship.[4]

The urge to assume a scheme of evolution and the suggestion that its laws govern man's religious consciousness are, as a rule,

4. Even one of the most critical and magisterial scholars of mysticism of our own time, Gershom G. Scholem, finds it necessary to preface his book on *Major Trends in Jewish Mysticism*, first ed., 1941 (New York: Schocken, 1961) with a brief outline of general religious awareness. Accordingly, mysticism becomes "a definite stage in the historical development of religion . . . connected with, and inseparable from a certain stage of the religious consciousness. It is also incompatible with certain other stages. . . ." (p. 7).

incompetent guides in the study of religion. They form an external scale of values and are dangerously seductive because of the safety they promise the student, who can take a stance apart from the materials and judge from there. It is the same problem we have seen earlier in the temptation in the study of myths: to invent methods that keep the object of study at arm's length (p. xii–xiv, 22, 35). In the study of mysticism, however, the danger is much greater, because here the documents reach *so much* higher than the most subtly schematic scholarly inventions. Even without sharp-witted evolutionistic doctrines, studies of mystics teem with pedantry. Certainly in the realm of mystical writings we should be on guard against evolutionisms.

11 ✣
Mysticism:
Histories
and Types

T HE OBVIOUS threat of an extraneous scheme of
development that posits the point of the investigator's
preference as the highest point is that it annihilates the
historical texture. This holds true also for mystical
phenomena, although mystics seem to be least dependent
on historical coincidence. When we say that mystics are
least dependent on history, we should complete this by
saying that they are least dependent on the traditions and
vicissitudes that make up the history of their contemporaries.
It would be totally mistaken to confuse the mystic's
craving for absolutes with a scheme of evolution the
student would like to impose on the data. Such a scheme

has as a rule little in common with the mystical documents, however much he admires them. It goes without saying that his criticism is not directed only at the many who have interpreted religious documents in the spell of Otto's reasonings. It is especially applicable to socioscientific tendencies (including those of a Marxist type) which duck the problem of history by substituting one line or dialectic of development which *im Groszen and Ganzen* remains unchanged. Self-criticism is mandatory for the student dependent only on his intellect in the study of documents that surpass that intellect considerably. Mystical documents especially demand a willingness toward self-criticism on our part. All external schematization here, whether it idealizes certain mystics as fortresses of faith or belittles them as products of a society not up to our own standards, has in common that it familiarizes us with the mystical documents prematurely by ignoring the new and singular things the documents might tell us.

Nor can mysticism be explained as merely the isolated experience of single individuals. Here too, the unusual cannot be "familiarized" by making it a case in a well-known general area, an "eccentricity" or a "pathology." Neither can mysticism be regarded the property of a certain period (stage of evolution) or culture. Disconcerting though it may be for our orientation in studying, the facts bear out the contention that "particularly coherent mystical experiences are possible at any and every degree of civilization and of religious situation."[1] Any hasty orientation is excluded, here as well as in the study of mythology. The statement that mysticism is attested in the most diverse circumstances is of course very different from the conclusion that it is everywhere the

1. Mircea Eliade, *Shamanism, Archaic Techniques of Ecstasy* (Bollingen Series LXXVI; New York: Pantheon, 1964), p. xix.

same. Such a conclusion is impossible here, as in the case of mythology.

The double problem of mysticism as a phenomenon in a great many different historical situations, yet showing certain similarities, is a problem for the erudite. It is inevitable, however, and to satisfy the learned some dry reasonings must follow here.

Mysticism occurs indeed in particular contexts, in particular historical settings and, we might say, to a certain degree as deviations from accepted myths. It is unusual to use the word mysticism in the plural. Maybe this linguistic circumstance has helped to create the common opinion that mystics are "as like as peas in a pod."[2] There are many mysticisms.

There were special historical circumstances in which Jewish mysticism was born and found its central expressions. Not only did it coincide with the growing Christian church, but there occurred at the same time the strange religious movement known as Gnosticism. This gnostic movement during the first few centuries after Christ constituted a major threat to the church, which felt compelled to formulate its "orthodoxy" not in the last place in reaction to this threat. "Gnosis" denotes that specific saving knowledge a man needs to attain his destination, which is realization of his identity with God. Gnosticism certainly has a mystical strain, but it is significant that Jewish mysticism kept itself free from its terminology. Crucial for gnostics were ideas of a divine fullness (*pleroma*) and wisdom (*sophia*). Jewish mystics did not use Greek concepts but seem to have kept their distance from pagan philosoph-

2. Expression by which Professor Elmer O'Brien gave a caricature of this common and mistaken opinion, in his *Varieties of Mystic Experience* (New York: Holt, 1964), p. 3.

ical terms by choosing biblical images. Central for them rather than the *pleroma* was God's throne-chariot (merkabah) spoken of in the book of Ezekiel.[3]

Christian mysticism was heir to paganism and its terminology in a manner Judaism was not. It spoke the "pagan" languages Greek and Latin, and behind the mysticism of an Augustine is the language of (neo)Platonism. Of course, this is not meant to belittle Augustine's Christianity and the biblical roots of his thought. Nevertheless, it is obvious that it makes a difference whether one addresses an audience nurtured by Greek philosophy or one already convinced of the authority of the Hebrew scriptures.

The greatest mystic of late Antiquity was the pagan Plotinus. He thought of himself as a true interpreter of Plato. His philosophical refinement not only provided concepts many later mystics used, but it served him in turning against the gnostics.

The period of late Antiquity, which witnessed the birth of neo-platonic mysticism, Gnosticism, Jewish mysticism, the rise of Christianity and Christian mysticism has among its characteristics the dwindling importance of traditional local cults, while the Roman Empire had created all the conditions for the propagation of foreign cults with new universal pretensions.

New religious problems arose in pious practices and for the intellect. To realize a truly divine presence in a confluence of cults and deities lost the self-evidence that the old cults possessed. History provided a strong stimulus for ideas of a much more individual and experiential gist. To realize a divine presence required novel purifications. Cultically the mystery-religions had

3. Gershom Scholem, *Major Trends in Jewish Mysticism*, pp. 42–44.

much to offer. Intellectually, gnostic teachings satisfied many. At the same time, it is understandable that mysticism could flourish more than ever.[4]

The concept of purification occurs in a great many mystical texts, but each age demands a new expression of it. Plotinus, living in that world of religious turmoil and himself nourished by the reading of Plato, spoke of purification in the clearest way. "Purified, the soul is wholly Idea and reason."[5] A person must turn away from all external objects and acquire a new manner of seeing. Then it can be said of him that "he is like one who, having penetrated the inner sanctuary, leaves the temple images behind him. . . ."[6] This does not mean that the cult images become insignificant. The world in general does not lose its meaning for Plotinus; he is not dualistic like the gnostics. The world is not ultimately despicable as it is for them, yet the period in which he lived lends special force to his simile.

For Plotinus, man is essentially an intellectual being. Plotinus is not the only mystic for whom Right Knowledge is in the center. One of the great Renaissance mystics, Nicholas of Cusa, often used mathematical models to illustrate his mystical expositions. In India, the towering figure is Śaṃkara (eighth century A.D.), a master of intellectual discourse.

Can we speak of historical conditionings to explain such preferences for knowledge? Only with the greatest prudence. It is

4. The classical book on this world and its quests is Eduard Norden, *Agnostos Theos* (first published in 1912; Stuttgart: Teubner, 1956). See especially pp. 109–115.

5. *Enneads* I, 6, 6 in Elmer O'Brien, *The Essential Plotinus* (New York: Mentor, 1964), p. 40.

6. *Enneads* VI, 9, 11. Translation Stephen Mac Kenna, *Plotinus: The Enneads* (London: Faber, 1956), p. 624.

possible to see the influence of the proverbial clarity of Greek thought in Plotinus. It is also possible to associate the general rebirth of Platonism and neo-Platonism with Nicholas of Cusa. Finally, it is clear that a relation exists between Śaṃkara's thought and the necessity for discussion with the intelligentsia of his Buddhist opponents, whose dialectical ability had been fostered for centuries in monasteries and academies. But no matter how one would like to arrive at an "objective," historical explanation, one must acknowledge the obvious individual gifts and talents that are not quite of the order of historical generalizations, as well as the obvious differences in the various "histories of ideas" behind them.

It never goes without saying that a mystic should concentrate his efforts on the intellect.

Next to concepts of an intellectual analysis, terms for love occur in abundance with equal or greater emphasis—love ranging from a tranquil absorption into a divine reality to ecstatic raptures. And again, historical considerations can illuminate features of a period, but not give a full explanation.

In India, a few centuries after Śaṃkara, Rāmānuja appears. He too is an intellectual giant, but the crucial factor in his mystical philosophy is the love for God and the grace bestowed by God on man. His thought sums up and bestows with a new intellectual status an earlier movement of wandering preachers and hymnologists who chanted the praises of God in the vernaculars of India. Of course, the pinnacle of love for God does not exclude the element of knowing; all of Rāmānuja's work is there to testify to that.

In Europe mysticisms of love blossomed too. It goes without saying that Christianity had its influences here and provided forms immediately inspired by the liturgy and by the prayer life of believers. The famous treatise by Augustine, the *Confessions*, is in fact a long prayer to God. A new impetus was provided by the lyrics of the medieval minnesingers. Their influence is not so hard to understand, since their praises of the beloved usually surpassed the ordinary human passions. The Flemish woman mystic, Hadewych (thirteenth century) sang of her ecstasy in the love of God, following the style of the minnesingers. God, or perhaps even better, the love of God is the beloved, not less mysterious, not less real:

> *I tell you that I love*
> *With my heart's blood.*
> *My senses wither in me*
> *In this rapture of love*
>
> . . . .
>
> *I suffer, I cannot go, I reach,*
> *My blood goes out to it*
> *I greet that sweet that will*
> *Relieve my ecstatic pain.*
>
> . . . .
>
> *Oh, Love, that I might be love*
> *To love thee with the love of Love!*
> *Oh Love, for Love's sake, make that I,*
> *Being love know Love fully as Love.*[7]

Another mystic, this time in the Islamic world, like Hadewych a woman and a visionary, became sick and was asked what the cause might be. She answered, "By God, I know of no cause

7. Approximate translation of some of the stanzas of one of Hadewych's poems (No. XV). Text in J. van Mierlo, S. J., *Hadewych, Een bloemlezing uit hare werken* (Amsterdam: Elsevier, 1950), pp. 269–271.

for my illness, except that Paradise was displayed to me, and I yearned after it in my heart; and I think that my Lord was jealous for me, and so reproached me; and only He can make me happy."[8] The woman, Rābi'a by name, is one of the early representatives of Sufism, famous for its glorification of divine love. Perhaps many movements of love-mysticism can be in part explained as a reaction against a theologizing that is felt to be too dry and too remote. This is certainly true of sufism, although here too more intellectual types of mysticism were well represented. For one thing, Plotinus had as much influence in the Islamic world as in the West.

The list of mysticisms of which historical researches inform us is endless. Long before Śaṃkara and Rāmānuja, India had its mystics whose teachings fill the Upaniṣads. These teachings were principally reinterpretations—or should we say, more refined interpretations—of sacred texts. To this extent there is a parallel with the mysticism of Jews, Christians, and Muslims. In all cases the mystic interpretations are presented as revelations of the real meaning of the text, whether the Vedas, the Old or New Testaments, or the Koran. This fact is fascinating all by itself and may cause a text-historian who is not too well disposed toward mystics to smile. But "It is the usual fate of sacred writings," wrote professor Scholem in his work on Jewish mysticism, "to become more or less divorced from the intentions of their authors."[9] And there was more wisdom of the true historian who knows his limits than despair in the words he added: "and after all—who knows what their original meaning was?"[10] Religion, and likewise mysticism,

8. A. J. Arberry, *Sufism, An Account of the Mystics of Islam* (London: Allen, 1956), p. 42.

9. Gershom G. Scholem, *Major Trends in Jewish Mysticism*, p. 14.

10. *Ibid.*

lives by reinterpretation. And often the reinterpretation acquires the greater importance. That was the case with the great Upaniṣadic reinterpretations of the Vedic texts.

The Upaniṣads were new interpretations of sacred texts, but this external description exhausts the similarity to many a Jewish or Christian mysticism. Those texts and the questions arising from them were altogether different. Among other things, the Upaniṣadic mysticism arose from a sense of puzzlement over the ritual; it was in relation to the ritual that the Vedic hymns were handed down. Some of the basic mystical terms owed their vitality to the ritual. One such term is *brahman*, the most famous name for "the Absolute." From of old, it was especially in the ritually efficacious stanzas (*mantras*) that the *brahman* resided.

It might seem from this list of mysticisms that mysticism is limited to the "great" historical traditions. Ethnological literature in all its diversity, however, has recorded many instances of religious behavior and expression that cannot be separated from the examples given here. That it adds another series of divergent contexts and sorts of mysticism can hardly come as a surprise. One of the great merits of the book by professor Eliade on Shamanism[11] is that it overcomes evolutionistic biases with the help of an astounding mass of facts from various "primitive" religions. Only a few decades ago, the word "shaman" was used as a synonym for witchdoctor and magician. In fact, the shaman is the expert in religious (and related medical) affairs in many archaic societies, such as those of the Siberian peoples and the North American Indians. In many cases, he is distinct from the regular priest. He

---

11. Mircea Eliade, *Shamanism.*

has a special calling and initiation. It is the shaman who is able to communicate with another world, guiding the souls of the dead or returning the souls of the sick. He is able to enter into an ecstasy and face what holds the world together. Hence Eliade speaks of "a concrete mystical experience." In the case of such mysticism, it is evident that there is not even a semblance of a "reaction" against commonly held opinions, and in that too the shaman is like many other mystics.

The shaman's activity is of paramount importance to the community as a whole. His help can make the hunt successful, since he knows how to implore the higher powers. But it is of the greatest significance that "what for the rest of the community remains a cosmological ideogram, for the shaman . . . becomes a mystical itinerary."[12]

It is quite obvious that not only are primitive traditions among themselves as variegated as the others, but also a sharp distinction exists in general between historical situations in which a mystic's authority is accepted and those in which he is branded as a deviationist or heretic. Historical investigations then make it quite difficult to generalize about mysticism.

Generalizations have their limits even if they are made in terms of the histories of ideas to which we have in the main restricted our observations. Things would become still more complex if political, social, and economic facts were added. But the sampling given will suffice. Obviously, there is a difference between the rapture of a Sūfī, a prayer of Augustine, and a shamanic seance in which a soul is conducted to heaven.

12. *Ibid.*, p. 265.

Even without giving too much weight to historical circumstances, *types* of mysticism can be distinguished.[13] They are distinguishable because of the difference in highest experiences the mystics themselves record. For some mystics the highest experience is of a "pantheistic" nature; an identification of the self with the cosmos is felt. The term "pantheism" suggests the involvement of God, and it would be more accurate, as Zaehner proposes, to speak of "pamphysistic" ("all nature") or a "pan-en-henic" (all-in-one) experience. This type is what most people commonly associate with mysticism. A romantically inspired popularization of religious facts is perhaps most responsible for this onesidedness. Pantheistic notions appealed to a great many Romantic writers who at the same time stimulated scholarly interest in religion. Goethe, who grew up with the German Romantic movement, remained a pantheist all his life.

Pantheism is by no means the only or the fundamental experience of the mystic. An experience of much greater importance for the history of mysticism in India can be denoted by the term "emancipation" or "isolation." The soul when purified finds its bliss in separation from the entanglements that make for the endless evolvements and changes of the world and which are responsible for the illusions constitutive of normal human lives. Such isolation of the soul by itself, no longer subject to time, differs fundamentally from the union implied in all pan-en-henic forms, whether a union with nature or with God.

Still another distinct type of mystical experience is of a strong

13. R. C. Zaehner, *Mysticism, Sacred and Profane* (New York: Oxford University Press, 1961) focuses on this problem of distinct types. He includes in his study artificially induced ecstasies, thereby drawing also on his own experiences with mescalin.

theistic character. The mystic feels absorbed in God, but the sensation of this absorption by itself makes less of an impression than the overwhelming sense that God is still more, infinitely more. Such overwhelming "forlornness" in God of course has its natural environment in traditions that emphasize God's grace, as the Viṣṇu traditions of South India, Christianity, and certain movements in Mahāyāana Buddhism and Islam.

With the subject of shamanism uppermost in our minds, it might be appropriate to add yet another type: the living experience of the mythological world in which the community as a whole has its orientation, an experience moreover that is felt as having its effect on the well-being of that community.

The problem of delineating types is made particularly difficult by one pronounced historical circumstance: mystics do not always attach the same importance to their experience. Quite famous is the passage of a letter in which the apostle Paul speaks of his mystical experiences, but does not derive his authority from them. Paul refers to himself in the third person, almost with an irony for his own boasting. He makes "a fool" of himself by doing it, he says, and would not have done so if his addressees (the Corinthian church) had not "forced" him to.

I must boast; there is nothing to be gained by it, but I will go on to visions and revelations of the Lord. I know a man in Christ who fourteen years ago was caught up to the third heaven—whether in the body or out of the body I do not know, God knows. And I know that this man was caught up into Paradise—whether in the body or out of the body I do not know, God knows—and he heard things that cannot be told, which man may not utter. On behalf of this man I will boast, but on my own behalf I will not boast, except of my weaknesses. Though if I wish to boast, I shall not be a fool, for I shall be speaking the truth. But I refrain from it, so that no one may think more of me than he sees in me or hears from me.[14]

The equally famous sequence tells us that he was given "a thorn in the flesh" with the special purpose to keep him "from being too elated by the abundance of revelations."

The description of this mysticism somehow recalls the last type listed. Indeed, here the reality is felt of what for the community seems only an "ideogram." Yet the context, presenting Paul's evaluation, makes it quite clear that for Paul any reveling in such visions would distract the attention from what *should* be the center of the Christian faith.

It should be borne in mind that the formulation of "types" has its dangers. For few of the formulated types occur as such in any historical setting. The mystics as we know about them show all sorts of "transitional" forms. These forms are nevertheless the real ones.

The formulation of types has one great advantage: it gives us a clearer and more comprehensive image of basic features in the manifold phenomenon of mysticism. Together with the samplings of historical contexts a typology may help us in avoiding pedantries. It clarifies what our lack of a definition means. Viewing various mystics side by side, we cannot very well measure and compare the truth and intensity of their experience. We might feel tempted to say of Augustine that he was only a part-time mystic compared to Plotinus. We might feel tempted to suggest that Plotinus really did not have as much of an experience of the divine truth as some truly ecstatic Sūfīs and that he developed his system of thought

14. II Cor. 12, 1–6 (R.S.V.).

more after his desire for mystical experience than in possession of it. But on the basis of the variety of types, such probings are meaningless. They suggest an objectivity that the data do not allow and betray a subjectivity on the part of the questioner that is usually not to the point.

The historian's findings at the root of any typology remain a warning. When summarized, they continue to be of a negative character: no mysticism ever lifts a man or a man's innermost being above all historical settings, traditions, and mythologies; not all ties can ever be severed between civilization and mystical expressions. Generalizing about relations between myth and mysticism we should have in mind relations between specific mystical expressions and their specific traditional contexts.

Finally, let us remember that most of the reasonings in this chapter served the questions of the erudite. To the wise, a word surely would have been enough. Perhaps the word of the Buddhist monk who said, "Now that I am enlightened, I am as miserable as ever." I believe the monk was Japanese. But he could have been something else. At any rate, I am sure he would not object if we substituted for "as miserable as ever": as Arabian as ever," "Jewish," "Christian," "sectarian," "ecstatic," or "as historical."

12 🌱
The Origin,
the Supreme,
Visible and
Invisible

M YSTICAL EXPERIENCE is expressed, no matter how immeasurable the height of the plane on which the mystic has it. Only the expressions can enable us to see how it relates to myth and its formation.

Considerable space is given to the mystery of "the beginning." To speak of the beginning implies in many texts speaking of "the one" and "the invisible," especially for mystics with a strong intellectual tendency. Nicholas of Cusa devoted a special treatise to the beginning (*De principio*). It is a little irony of history that he takes as his starting point a New Testament line from the Vulgate that misinterpreted the Greek text.

In a discussion with the Jews who ask him who he is, Jesus answers, "Why should I speak to you at all?" Another possible understanding is, "I am what I have told you all along." (Thus the King James Version: "Even the same that I said unto you from the beginning.") But Nicholas took the Vulgate text and understood: "Who are you? Jesus answered them: the Origin, and as such I speak to you." (Principium qui et loquor vobis.) Remembering the wisdom of professor Scholem, however, that reinterpretations of sacred books can outweigh the earlier meaning, and that moreover we may not be so clear as to the earliest intention, we should not be overbearing with historical criticism here. The mystery of the Origin Cusanus has in mind is of a different order from a textual starting point. These are his first sentences:

With God's help, I propose to say something about the subject of the Origin, by way of training for the intellect. The word "origin"[1] is a feminine in Greek and has the accusative in this place. Hence Augustine interprets: "Believe in me as the one who speaks to you as the Origin, so that you will not perish in your sins." So let us first examine whether there is an origin.[2]

Invoking a commentary (by Proclus) on Plato, Cusanus expounds that whatever is divisible is dependent on something else. What is properly called "origin" must be totally independent; it cannot be divided, nor can it cease to be. Thus the question of the origin is identical with that of perfect being, the ultimate ground of all things.

1. *archè*
2. I use the text edited by Leo Gabriel (with German translation by Dietlind and Wilhelm Dupré), *Nikolaus von Kues, Philosophisch-Theologische Schriften* (Vienna: Herder, 1966), Vol. II.

Further, every visible datum is active by means of an invisible power, as fire by heat, snow by coldness. Generally the factor which acts and generates is invisible. However, in that which subsists through itself, doing and what is done, producing and produced is the same. Hence, it is not visible.

It is not necessary to attempt a summary of Cusanus' or any other great mystic's thought. It suffices to notice in this perfectly intellectual exposition the expression of "the beginning" and the association with invisibility. Both notions irresistibly remind one of the myths of origins with which we began our discussion. There too we found the "ground" of the world depicted as different from whatever is ordinarily visible. At the same time, there is a striking difference. The mystic begins his discourse with the clear consciousness that it is like a *training for the intellect*. This is not to be understood as "gymnastics." It is a conscious effort to arrive at that unity wherein the universe with all its conflicts becomes transparent. Cusanus himself coined the famous word "coincidentia oppositorum," the union of opposites. It is as if the whole creation as it appears to man must be traversed in a reverse order. The lengthy reasonings and the intellectual rigor they demand—not excluding but implying experience—make the texts of a Cusanus quite different from the majority of creation myths. The latter can be listened to with a less intense effort; often the dramatic quality is enough to keep one spellbound.

Concepts of invisibility describe "the highest" in many texts. Sanskrit is a much more precise language in the description of problems of knowledge and experience than Latin or any modern Western language. The celebrated Hindu song the Bhagavadgītā presents a choice list of words for the Supreme. Its opening scene is an enlarged picture of human anxieties. The hero Arjuna is about to engage in the great battle of Kurukṣetra, in which duty will compel him to slay many friends and kinsmen. He tells Kṛṣṇa his doubts concerning the rightness and meaning of such duty. And immediately Kṛṣṇa, the divine teacher, begins to speak of the basis of these doubts and anxieties. It is the confusion of what is eternal and what is not eternal.

The question what or who is "the eternal one" or "supreme one" is not easy to explain. Part of the difficulty for us is that Sanskrit is wealthy in nuances for problems relating to knowledge-and-experience. Rendering these nuances in any of our Western languages inevitably results in cumbersome circumscriptions. The problem of different histories of ideas becomes acute.

It is necessary to realize that the Bhagavadgītā gained an appeal much wider than any mystical text in the West has ever had. Ideas akin to the notion of "invisibility" can illustrate this point. The word *avyakta* is variously translated as "unmanifest," "unobservable," or "undifferentiated." Kṛṣṇa teaches Arjuna that the Supreme is "unmanifest," as well as unthinkable and not subject to change (Bhagavadgītā II 25). The notion of invisibility is not so hard to grasp in the traditions of Hinduism as it would be for most of us. Every Hindu knows temples in which a god or goddess is depicted, yet he would never confuse the image with the deity's reality. Also, without having studied philosophy, he knows that that reality is somehow behind or beyond the image. By contrast and for various reasons, the Christian tradition has always thought of the reality of God as having revealed itself "in history." Moreover, the events in which this happened became the center of all teachings. It is needless to add that this interest in events, *doings* of God, is associated most with concerns about the *will* of God, more so than about His presence. God's presence in events manifests His will.

Of course, this difference between East and West is a difference of emphasis. In the West too, the presence of God plays its role. Particularly the mystics absorbed in God's *love* have felt His presence above all in the liturgy of the church. Among them is Hadewych. Often it is her "receiving of the Lord"—in the communion celebration—that seems to set off her mystical experience. And also for mystics of a very different sort, such as Ignatius of Loyola, the dynamic founder of the order of the Jesuits, the presence of the Lord in the liturgy is as real as His will. But the difference in central concerns of Hindu and Christian traditions is not reduced. The manner of God's presence in the life and work of Jesus Christ became hotly disputed at an early time. Later, the manner of his presence in the communion constituted a problem for which carefully worded, doctrinal formulations had to be devised. The Protestant movement continued and in some ways complicated the picture. The reformed churches denied the presence of the Lord apart from the act of the communion celebration itself. From a Hindu point of view, one could say that in this whole Christian development the self-evidence of God's presence had faded. It is not hard to understand in this context how in Christianity—and likewise in Judaism and Islam—mystical experience could come to be regarded at times as a foreign or even inimical element. I do not think that words like *avyakta* in the Bhagavadgītā have had the strange sound that even the word "invisible" as used by Nicholas of Cusa has for us.

When Kṛṣṇa begins his instruction about the one who is unmanifest, he does not take the trouble to make very clear what or who this *one* is. One can sense that Cusanus, broaching the subject of the Origin, will speak of God on the next page, as indeed he does. Scripture is quoted to make clear that the real meaning of the tradition is being uncovered. In Kṛṣṇa's teachings the meaning of certain *traditions* has its part, but much more striking is the exposition of the principal *problem:* the confusion of what is eternal and what is not eternal. Comparatively speaking, the vindication of the mystical convictions has a much less conspicuous role here. In the face of Arjuna's—and we should add, all men's—anxiety, Kṛṣṇa points out a distinction between all "these bodies" of the people who are to engage in battle and "the one that has a body" (śarīrin, II,18). The former will "come to an end," but the latter is "said to be eternal, imperishable and immeasurable" (II,18). It would not be right to substitute our word "soul" for this "embodied one." The idea of "one soul in all bodies" certainly found adherents in Indian philosophy, but it is as if the author of the Song purposely chose a word without too much scholastic precision. (The whole text of the Bhagavadgītā presents the problem to most Western readers that no one single system of thought is opted for to the exclusion of others.) That Kṛṣṇa's concern is to overcome men's basic confusion is clear from what follows. The mysterious śarīrin is not mentioned anymore, but the qualifications given him (for the word is a masculine) sound most like a hymn of praise to a God.

> *When someone thinks of him as slaying*
> *or someone thinks he is one who can be killed*
> *Both are devoid of understanding*
> *He does not kill and is not killed.*
> *He is not born and does not die*
> *Nor did he ever come to be nor will he cease to be.*

He is unborn, subsisting in himself, ancient, and everlasting.
    The body will be slain, but he will not.

. . . .

He cannot be cut and cannot be burned,
    not moistened and not dried
Subsisting always everywhere, immobile,
    fixed is the eternal one.
He is unmanifest (avyakta), unthinkable and not
    subject to change. Thus he is said to be.
Therefore, once you have understood him in this way,
    lamenting him is not befitting you.[3]

As we saw, Cusanus drew on worldly examples to make a discussion of invisibility possible: fire and snow have their properties through an invisible power. Is it correct to draw conclusions next about the nature of God? No doubt, we have our difficulties in following the reasonings of mystics especially at this point. However, the range of the word *avyakta* (and its greater openness for common understanding) enabled the author of the Bhagavadgītā to approach the problem of invisibility in a manner that can even facilitate our own understanding. The text of the Bhagavadgītā (in accordance with virtually all "orthodox" Indian traditions) holds to a conviction already expressed in the Vedic texts, that the supreme being causing the world to arise, while being identical with the material cause of the world, supersedes the world by far. In other words, there is no "simple pantheism." One famous Vedic hymn describes in unmistakable mythological terms the primeval sacrifice performed by the gods, from which the world is born. After briefly depicting the Puruṣa, the giant-like

3. Bhagavadgītā II, 19, 20, 24, 25.

being that serves as the sacrificial victim, which "is all this, both what has been and what will be," the hymn says:

> Such is his greatness, and more than that is Puruṣa.
> A fourth of him is all beings, three fourths of him is
>   what is immortal in heaven.[4]

This ancient conviction is recognizably continued in the Bhagavadgītā:

> This whole world is stretched out (or pervaded)
>   by Me in the form of the Unmanifest (avyakta).
> All beings rest in Me
>   but I am not exhausted in them.[5]

It is in line with this that the Gītā distinguishes "levels" of *avyakta*.[6] The unmanifestness of God in which all perishable beings reside is only one level on which the divine being is unmanifest.

> From the unmanifest all manifestations take their birth . . .
> And . . . disappear in that same one known as the unmanifest.[7]

A higher level of unmanifestness is that of the supreme one's *total* reality:

4. Ṛgveda X, 90, translation A. A. MacDonell, *A Vedic Reader* (London: Oxford University Press, 1917), pp. 196–197.
5. Bhagavadgītā IX, 4.
6. A lucid discussion of "Avyakta and Brahman" is given by Surendranath Dasgupta, *A History of Indian Philosophy* (Cambridge: University Press, 1952), II, 470–479.
7. Bhagavadgītā VIII, 18.

*But higher than this unmanifest is another, an eternal unmanifest
That does not come to an end when all beings perish.*[8]

It is the Lord who is unmanifest in this sense who is the "highest
goal"[9] for man. Thus a mystical philosophy of levels of unmanifestness extends an accepted religious tradition. The existing articulation of transcendence-and-immanence-in-one did not call for
an antithesis. It is possible to understand that texts of an out-
spoken mystical character could become *popular* in India.

8. *Ibid.*, VIII, 20.
9. *Ibid.*, VIII, 21.

13 ❦
Mystical
Knowledge

FTER THESE examples of mystical terms relating to the origin
or the supreme Lord, the observation cannot be repressed
that the knowledge required on the mystical path is
knowledge of a peculiar sort and lays peculiar demands on
a person. All mystics have always been aware of the
peculiarity of mystical knowledge and its requirements.
This is equally true in Indian situations where mystical
forms were accepted whole-heartedly.

Perhaps the acceptance of mysticism to some extent as
normal in India enabled mystics to introduce the
requirements for their knowledge in a more down-to-earth
manner than in the West. Śaṃkara, beginning his famous

commentary on the Vedāntasūtras (1.1.1), lists the antecedent conditions for the study of Brahman. The first is a "sense of discrimination of things that are permanent and things that are impermanent" (*nityānityavastu-viveka*). Not everyone has this sufficiently and the attitude that should go with it: "the renunciation of all desire to enjoy the fruits (of one's actions) both here and hereafter; the acquirement of tranquility, self-restraint, . . . and the desire of final release."[1] Śaṃkara realizes that an enquiry into Brahman is commonly preceded by a study of religious duties, which implies the study of the early Vedic texts. However, he lists his prerequisites in opposition to other thinkers who insist on such an earlier study as the principal foundation for an enquiry into Brahman. The discussions he engages in and the discussions for centuries after him are another example of a problem in mystical writings easier to discern in India than in the West. For at every point it is akin to the question, is mystical knowledge based on scriptural authority or is its source somewhere else?

We should abstain from discussing the complexities in the debate between Śaṃkara's followers and Rāmānuja, his principal opponent, with his followers. In the latter circles Śaṃkara was often called a crypto-Buddhist, since he did not seem to accept the authority of the Vedas, at least not completely. It is important for the relationship of mysticism to mythology not only that the problem of knowledge was crucial for mystics, but that no mystical point of view ever provided a final answer. Indeed, no answer provided seemed to satisfy other mystics in the same general tradition.

    1. Frans George Thibaut, *The Vedānta Sūtras of Bādarāyana with the commentary by Śaṅkara* (Sacred Books of the East, Vol. XXXIV, Oxford: Clarendon Press, 1890 [Reprinted New York: Dover, 1962]), I, 12.

Rāmānuja himself, with the arguments of Śaṃkara in mind, arrived at several emphatic formulations concerning the source of mystical experience. For instance,

That of which scripture is the womb, the cause, and the source of knowledge, that is the brahman (and can therefore be spoken of as that) which has scripture as its womb and source. Scripture is the womb to the extent that it is the cause of the insight into the brahman.[2]

The brahman, he continues, is not within the reach of any other body of knowledge. Hence, the study of religious duty must not be belittled in any way.

From a nonmystic viewpoint—or should we say from the viewpoint of an ordinary mythology?—the mystical formulations about knowledge seem to show a certain circularity. On one hand, the ability to know is a property of man, though some have it more than others. On the other hand, mystical knowledge leads beyond knowledge—yet there alone all the rest becomes transparent.

Although it may be argued that the "ordinary" mythological traditions also show a peculiar logic (a well-known example is the story of Genesis 1, narrating the creation of light before the sun and moon, and the assignment of "every green plant for food . . . to every beast of the earth") the seriousness of many mystical argumentations and their insistence on consistency make the

2. After the translation of A. Hohenberger, *Rāmānuja's Vedāntadīpa, seine kurze Auslegung der Brahmasūtren des Bādarāyaṇa*, Bonner Orientalische Studien, Vol. 14, ed. Otto Spies (Bonn: Selbstverlag des Orientalischen Seminars der Universität Bonn, 1964), p. 3.

peculiarity of their logic conspicuous. I suggest that we do not call it circularity. Such a judgment would make no sense in the reading of myths, and chances are that it makes no sense in the understanding of mysticism. For the sake of description, "self-containment" will be a better word. Certain premises are made about what we might call the first 180 degrees of the circle of knowledge, such as the certainty of Rāmānuja about scriptural revelation. These premises may articulate or overarticulate traditional data; they are somehow at variance with what the majority had thought so far. If those premises are only slightly different from another mystic's, conflicts seem inevitable.

Civilizations adamant on convictions about religious authority stimulate conflict situations. In India, martyrs are the exception, even among those—unlike Śaṃkara!—who rejected the value of the Vedic tradition completely. The history of the Islamic and Christian mystics is different. Among the most famous mystics is the Muslim al-Halladj, who was executed in 922 in Bagdad. He had been imprisoned for years, was tortured, finally decapitated, and afterwards burned. He had denied the binding power of the prescribed ritual duties.[3] The verdict was inevitable, the case clearcut. A prayer of al-Halladj is recorded in which he would have said, "Thy presence is knowledge—not tradition."[4]

The most talked-about Christian mystic whose views did not please the church in his days is Eckhart. In a few sentences about him one would hesitate to use the heavy word "knowledge." For he was not only a systematic thinker, but an eminent preacher, able to express his thought in disarmingly simple and direct ways.

3. A. J. Wensinck, *Oostersche Mystiek, Christelijke en Mohammedaansche* (Amsterdam: Paris, 1930), pp. 61–72.
4. *Ibid.*, p. 67.

Men must throw down the lumber with which they load themselves—including their undue concern for learning. Man's soul, they will discover, is by nature akin to God. The "ground" of the soul is divine. Eckhart's imagery has the directness of natural events. Rather than of the process of mystical knowledge, he speaks of the *growth* of God in man. The most quoted expression by Eckhart is that of "God's birth in the soul." That is the content of many of his sermons. It means that Jesus Christ's existence loses some of its temporal, historical significance and appears as eternal. And, like Nicholas of Cusa after him, Eckhart was able to read many biblical texts in this manner. The daring simplicity of his expressions was more than the archbishop of Cologne could take, and several actions finally resulted in Eckhart's condemnation, worded in a papal bull. Part of the charge was that Eckhart wanted to know more than others, had lost himself in various unaccepted doctrines and brought darkness over the faith of simple believers.[5] Eckhart died before the bull was published.

Of course, neither in Islam nor in Christianity was there ever a persecution of mysticism as such. In both, the vast majority of mystics could express themselves within the limits of orthodoxy. Many could speak of their mystical knowledge and even propagate mystical views. This is not merely because of the variety of mysticism, but also because of times and circumstances, and whether the orthodoxy is flourishing or feels endangered. Nicholas of Cusa was an important church official and a zealous student of Eckhart's writings, in spite of their condemnation. Bernard of Clairvaux is one of many mystics sanctified by the church. It may

5. Joseph Quint (ed., trans.), *Meister Eckhart, Deutsche Predigten und Traktate* (München: Hanser Verlag, 1955), p. 449. Text in Denzinger, 501ff.; cf. Walter Nigg, *Das Buch der Ketzer* (Zürich: Artemis-Verlag, 1949), p. 277.

be said that he was not only a very different sort from either Eckhart or Cusanus, but managed to combine his ecstasies of love for Jesus and raptures in the passion story with an active career as church politician.

For our purposes, the mystical expressions of knowledge are striking because of their historical variety, but above all because the mystic is fully aware of the uniqueness of his knowledge. Compared with myth, the seriousness stands out with which the mystic engages in questions this knowledge evokes. These questions may differ from age to age, from culture to culture; the mystic devotes himself to them fully.

It would be jumping to conclusions if we thought of the mystic's problems with knowledge only in terms of the questions we can most easily discern: questions arising from individual logical ability and from an environment formulating its doubts in a more or less doctrinal fashion. The shamanic mystic has his full share of problems, and, like other mystics, is fully aware of the peculiarity of his knowledge.

In his remarkable book *Primitive Man as Philosopher*, Paul Radin made a broad and sensible distinction between two types of people present in all societies. There are men of action whose temperament is mainly of a practical nature, and, always less numerous, the thinkers, who are more given to contemplation.[6] The second are more difficult to categorize, no doubt. Yet, it can hardly be contended that if we do classify, the mystics belong here. There is a mystical strain in a Maori poem Radin cites to illustrate the nature of contemplative thought.

6. Paul Radin, *Primitive Man as Philosopher* (first published 1927; enlarged ed. New York: Dover, 1957), Chap. XIII.

Seeking, earnestly seeking in the gloom. Searching—yes on the coast line—on the bounds of night and day; looking into night. Night had conceived the seed of night. The heart, the foundation of night, had stood forth self-existing even in the gloom. It grows in gloom—the sap and succulent parts, the life pulsating, and the cup of life. The shadows screen the faintest ray of light. The pro-creative power, the ecstasy of life first known, and joy of issuing forth from silence into sound. Thus the progeny of the Great-Extending filled the heaven's expanse; the chorus of life rose and swelled into ecstasy, then rested in bliss of calm and quiet.[7]

The element of a personal quest is clearly suggested and strengthens the association with mysticism. Perhaps it is not too far-fetched to consider the poem's conciseness and think of the Vedāntasūtras, the brief lines meant for memorization, on which Śaṃkara and Rāmānuja built their elaborate systems. But also, as in mystical texts of the "great traditions," the personal element is not an individual isolation of opinions. The words rendered as "growing," "gloom," "ecstasy," "searching," "calm and "quiet," "heart," "self-existing," and the composition as a whole show an interest that is objective in intent. Radin rightly speaks of an "urge toward analysis and synthesis."[8] Certainly, the knowledge represented in this poem is awe-inspiring, even if it does not follow the rules of logic and observation with which the majority of "practical men" is satisfied.

Many a myth speaks of suffering and death, and the mystic's knowledge is frequently connected with disastrous experiences.

---

7. J. C. Andersen, *Maori Life in Aotea*, p. 150, quoted in Radin, *op. cit.*, pp. 237–238.

8. Radin, *op. cit.*, p. 237.

"The dark night of the soul" is an indispensable topic in studies of Western mysticism: "Impotence, blankness, solitude are the epithets by which those immersed in this dark fire of purification describe their pains," Evelyn Underhill writes in her study of mysticism.[9] The purification necessary in all mysticism is hardly ever painless. If we are justified in speaking of mystical *additions* to the "ordinary" mythological knowledge, we should reckon also with a shift of the center of knowledge. From the mystic's point of view "ordinary" mythological knowledge of suffering and death shows itself in a different perspective.

The documentation of mystics' "suffering" cannot lead to a generalization about mystical knowledge. The documentation is one more reminder that we have to deal with "deviations" *from specific* mythological traditions. As indicated in the statement by Evelyn Underhill, Western mysticism has a certain homogeneity when it comes to descriptions of the purification process. No matter how cautiously such a statement should be made, it also seems valid when we look at a very different type of civilization and its expressions for the sufferings that change a man's orientation. In cultures in which shamanism and shamanic mysticism function the expressions are strikingly more concrete. Although terrible mystical visions certainly occur in Western history, the "dark night of the soul" has an almost pale allegorical quality when compared to many a primitive experience of dread. An eighteenth-century traveler reported on the making of a medicine man among the Port Jackson tribes (Australia). Sleeping on a grave was part of it. There "The spirit of the deceased would visit him, seize him by

9. *Mysticism, A Study in the Nature and Development of Man's Spiritual Consciousness* (New York: Meridian, 1955), p. 381

the throat, and opening him, take out his bowels, which he replaced, and the wound closed up."[10]

All studies of shamanism mention events of this nature: initiatory sicknesses and dismemberment, an unmistakable experience of death.[11] The Bororo shamans (South America) sometimes receive the call to their new state from a spirit of the dead. The shaman-elect

walks in the forest and suddenly sees a bird perching within the reach of his hand and disappearing at once. Flocks of parrots come down to him and vanish as if by magic. The future shaman goes home, shaking and uttering unintelligible words. His body gives off a smell of putrefaction and moldiness. Suddenly, a gust of wind makes him stumble: he collapses as if dead. At this moment he becomes the receptacle of a spirit who speaks through his mouth. From this moment he is a shaman.[12]

Without revelations like these and such experience of death the secret knowledge cannot be imparted.

It is tempting for a "modern" man to shake his head and say that such things would not be taken so literally, for the initiatory trials, including death, are always and evidently followed by life. This is not the place to analyze the temptations of a modern mythology of sobriety. The point is that the concrete expressions of purification among "the primitives" owe as much to the various preceding mythologies as the Western mystical expressions owe to

10. A. W. Howitt, *The Native Tribes of South-East Australia*, p. 405. Quoted in M. Eliade, *Shamanism*, p. 45.

11. See M. Eliade, *Shamanism*, Chap. II, with elaborate bibliographical notes.

12. Alfred Métraux, "Le shamanisme chez les Indiens de l'Amérique du Sud tropicale," *Acta Americana* II, No. 3 (1944), 203.

their philosophical and religious backgrounds. But within their own traditions and the vocabularies they provide, "civilized" and "primitive" mystics give an expression to the uniqueness of the new knowledge they gain. Each in his own way, in terms that one could not adequately render in terms of another civilization and its esoteric knowledge, the mystic insists on this novelty.

14 ❦
Universality; Beyond the Official Tradition

I N   S O M E   cases, it is not enough to say of a mystic that he is at variance with his tradition, that his function in certain societies sets him apart from others, and that more is expected from him; it is not even sufficient to speak of an addition to the dominant mythology or of a shift in the central focus of knowledge. It seems to me that sometimes we see the mystic very definitely *surpass* the tradition in his expressions. He arrives at an experience of universality that his environment is not aware of or that his historical phase has lost. I think the following two examples are revealing as mystical steps beyond an accepted tradition. It is not a coincidence that both come from periods and environments of religious upheavals and "acculturation," where there is a dire intensification of the need for a "universal consciousness."

Augustine's gropings for a stable notion of universal import are well known from his *Confessions*. He had gone through philosophical struggles long before his conversion to Christianity. With hindsight we can see in his conversion the conversion of some of the strongest elements of classical culture. The God of the Christians to whom he finally bowed could not have meant anything to Augustine if He had not overwhelmed him with that universality he longed for. It may be unusual to call attention to this fact, evident as it is from every page of the *Confessions*. A move "beyond the tradition" such as Augustine's of course cannot mean a distortion of that tradition. Yet only such a pregnant expression can do some justice to the powerful personal experience that left an imprint on the Western church. The universality of God may have had its antecedents in various ways in the biblical texts—the prophets, the psalms, and the Pauline epistles—it took a new man to experience and express this universality in a new age, not only recognizing anew the biblical passages, but utilizing the tools of thought inherited from the classics. In this light we may see his writings, his vision of history in, and also as, *The City of God*, and at the same time the *Confessions*. The latter, as an autobiographical account in the form of a prayer, opens up the inner details of his life to Him who is the universal power in this microcosmos of individual existence as well as in the world at large. Few have been able to speak so directly about God's irresistible grace.

this man, bearing about his own mortality with him, carrying about him a testimony of his own sin . . . yet this man, this part of what thou hast created, is desirous to praise thee; thou so provokest him, that he even delighteth to praise thee. For thou hast created us for thyself, and our heart cannot be quieted till it may find repose in thee.[1]

A universal vision, encompassing and reintegrating the details of an inner life, can be accounted for only slightly by history. Thus we can group Augustine together with the small number of extraordinary men who came from outside or from the fringes of a great tradition and expressed most clearly its universal meaning— like Saint Paul, or like Śākyamuni the Buddha in Indian spirituality. The new image of man and the religious orientation affected by such a giant is more than any of his contemporaries had been able to experience and express. It is also considerably more than historical investigation can weave together from the isolated strains before him.

The second example is one of less far-reaching consequences, or rather, one whose type we are not yet well enough able to recognize. It is the report on a mystical experience of a Japanese woman in our century.[2] By the time she wrote her experiences down, she had become a convert to the Roman Catholic church and a nun. It was at the request of her superiors that she gave her account. In the letter with her account, she writes,

I am happy, sincerely, when in accordance with your knowledge, you offer a prayer of thanks for God's infinite compassion and His profound love for this little creature and when you pray for the for-

---

1. Trans. William Watts (1631), in *St. Augustine's Confessions* (Loeb Classical Library; Cambridge: Harvard University Press, 1950), I, 3.

2. See Heinrich Dumoulin, *Ostliche Meditation und christliche Mystik* (Freiburg: Verlag Karl Alber, 1966), Appendix B, pp. 308–328.

giveness of my infidelities. *I have not paid any attention to such things as style, but written just as it came to me. Please, excuse me for my inept way of writing. If you find anything false in my soul I ask you for the love of the Lord to enlighten me. In humility, I leave everything to your right judgment and I wish only to follow your guidance with a joyful heart.*[3]

In lines like these, one might suspect some influence of Western mystical literature, with which the writer had become familiar. The lines are reminiscent, for instance, of Teresa of Avila in her autobiography. Teresa, too, four centuries ago, wrote lines imploring her superiors to rectify all mistakes, not only of her improper writing, but of her experience and thought. Nevertheless, together with this humility goes an absolute certainty of the things revealed in her mysticism.

The account of the Japanese nun arouses our interest since the experience it describes took place long before she knew about Christianity. The experience ruling her life is not only (to the extent that we can classify these matters) beyond the ordinary and tangible Christian tradition, but in the ordinary course of events outside of it.

She was born in an aristocratic family closely associated with the emperor's court. Ancestral functions and customs tied her to the mythical past of Japan. The monastic life she knew about as a child and which stimulated her childish longings for purity was that of Buddhism.

Then, at the age of eleven or twelve, she has the crucial experience of her life in the garden of her family home. While watching the evening sky, she writes,

3. Dumoulin, p. 309.

an unspeakable bright, very bright, radiant light shone forth at one corner of the sky. It enveloped my little self completely, it also enveloped the whole garden around me, it filled the whole area and radiated bright and sublime. It was as if my own little person was powerfully drawn into this powerful light. Unconscious and immobilized, I gazed at this light, spellbound. Oh, this light, that which was behind this light, was so ineffably exalted that I cannot describe it with words—it was high, pure, full of some indelible, absolute majesty. My little self, oblivious of itself, could only gaze at it. How long it lasted—I remember no notion of the time of it. Human words are incapable of rendering the impression I received through it. And the impression did not belong to the senses in any way, it was indescribable in form or words, it had no discernible shape at all. The profound impression and the certainty that were left on the ground of my soul are just as vivid now, after almost thirty years have gone by, as they were then. They are unchanged and have left such a profound certitude in me, that I cannot deny them.[4]

From this day on, the girl's life is transformed. Common human relationships have lost their value for her. She must devote herself to that power she experienced. She speaks of it in her account as a love that causes everything else to dwindle.

At the same time I understood by intuition that this whole world was ruled by this exalted being, this exalted one existing beyond the whole universe, this indelible, absolute being.[5]

4. Dumoulin, pp. 313–314.
5. Dumoulin, p. 314.

Her experience of this majestic authority is completed by

*the uninterrupted awareness, that this nothing, to wit, I myself,
continually receives its existence from this exalted being. This
awareness has never left me from then on till now.*[6]

One would like to know in detail how this certainty became
integrated in her life after her conversion and in her spiritual
progress in the convent. But the account as we have it is abridged
in the narration of those events. Even so, expressions used in the
abridged account do not suggest an articulation like Augustine's.
Some years after her great experience her sister invites her to some
religious meetings or exercises (the nature of which is not further
indicated than by saying that this sister was unhappy and searched
for help in them). Rather disarmingly, the girl declined the invita-
tion "because, apart from superstition, I had not heard of any
religious practice."[7] The conversion story is introduced with the
sentence: "With the true religion I came in touch only in 1919
or 1920."[8] The reader is not struck by any struggle for integration.

Granted that the sophistication of the document is not overwhelming, the point that has our interest is very clear in it. The
reality of her experience remains somehow beyond the tradition
she embraces. When she receives her Christian instruction, she
notes,

*God was not a stranger for me. He seemed to be the explanation for
that childhood event in the garden, which in my heart I always
called "the great God of the Garden" . . . The explanation about*

6. *Id.*
7. Dumoulin, p. 315.
8. Dumoulin, p. 315.

God did not mean any new revelation for me; it was only like an affirmation.[9]

Some time after her baptism, she reads the autobiography of St. Teresa of Avila. She writes that her heart was particularly moved when the Saint spoke of God's majesty.[10] Here too, she found an affirmation, not something new.

The expressions used by this modern woman mystic are quite similar to those used by Augustine in narrating his crucial mystical experience (*Confessions* VII, 10).[11] Augustine saw a light, as our mystic described, a light filling everything, but different from all other lights. With this came the experience of God's majesty, the source from which everything comes. Augustine learns in the experience—borrowing for his description from the psalmist[12]—that God chastises man with rebukes for his guilt and has the sensation that God makes his soul "consume away like a moth" (tabescere fecisti sicut araneam animam meam). Troubled by the nature of the truth he experiences in this indescribable manner, he hears the voice of God speaking the biblical word from Exodus 3: "I am that I am."

The strange light, the ineffability of the truth revealed, the awareness of divine authority and the dependence of all that is on this divine power make the descriptions of both preconversion experiences quite similar. For all these similarities, no one will suggest that the mysticism of both is the same. The difference between the nun and the great theologian remains. The great theo-

9. Dumoulin, p. 316.
10. Dumoulin, p. 317.
11. Cf. Dumoulin, p. 310.
12. Psalm 39, 11.

logian drew on his intellectual arsenal and the intellectual equipment of his time to integrate and evaluate his experience with precision. But each in his way illustrates the same point of importance: in the experience something beyond the official tradition is revealed. *It cannot be submerged in that tradition without transforming it.* Whether the novelty of the experience becomes realized indeed in the tradition depends on its magnitude and on the course of history. Needless to add, it also depends on the place in history from which we view events. With respect to Augustine's experience beyond Christianity, history has provided us with some perspective; in the case of the Japanese nun, it has not.

15 ✸
*Creative
Allegorization
and New
Symbols*

T O T A K E up the data of a mythology and renew them is
not an everyday affair. Nowhere is this clearer than in the
use mystics can make of "allegory."

   We have already seen some mystical allegorization in
the use made of texts from sacred scriptures. The interpretations of biblical texts Nicholas of Cusa or Eckhart arrived
at not only make the critical historian shake his head; more
generally even, they seem to be in conflict with common
sense. The tendency to see an infinite meaning in commonly
accepted traditions is so widespread in mystical documents
that it will be worthwhile to look at one more example
with special care.

159

The *Mahāprajñāpāramitāśāstra* ("Treatise on the Great Virtue of Wisdom") is a famous Buddhist philosophical work. Its author, Nāgārjuna, follows the Indian tradition of presenting his system in the form of a commentary on a basic text. This text is a *sūtra*. In the discussion of "subjective reservedness" as a characteristic of myth, we already mentioned the stylized opening formula in this type of literature: "Thus I have heard . . ." (p. 59). In the same manner the *sūtra* basic to Nāgārjuna's exposition begins: *Evam mayā śrutam ekasmin samaye.* Thus I heard at a certain occasion. After a long introduction Nāgārjuna arrives at this opening sentence, and takes up these very simple words one by one. We are shown the profound meaning of each.

Nāgārjuna explicitly raises the question: "Why do the Buddhist *sūtras* begin with the word *evam*, "thus"?[1] And this is part of his elaborate answer:

The Law of the Buddha (buddhadharma) *is a vast ocean. Confidence* (śraddhā) *is the beginning of the crossing of this ocean. Knowledge is that which crosses. Evam is synonymous with confidence. The man whose heart is full of pure confidence* (śraddhā-viśuddhi) *can enter the Law of the Buddha; without this confidence, he cannot. The man without confidence says:* "It is not thus (*it is not* evam);" *this characterizes incredulity* (aśrāddhya). *He who believes says:* "It is thus (evam etat)." *. . . the Buddha said:* "If a man has confidence, he can go into the sea of my great Law and gain the fruit of the religious life; it is not in vain that he shaves his head and puts on the monk's garment. If he has no confidence, he

1. Etienne Lamotte, *Le traité de la grande vertu de sagesse de Nāgārjuna* (*Mahāprajñāparamitāśāstra*) (Bibliothèque du Muséon, Vol. 18; Louvain: Bureaux du Muséon, 1944), Vol. I, Chap. II.

cannot go into the sea of my Law. Like a rotten tree which yields neither flowers nor fruits, he does not gain the fruit of the religious life. He can shave his head, put on the garments, study all sorts of sūtras and śāstras, he does not profit at all from the Buddhist Law." Therefore the word Evam occurs at the beginning of the Buddhist texts: it refers to that confidence.[2]

The logic of Nāgārjuna's interpretation is incontestable. Even the earliest Buddhist texts have made much of the first step to be taken. *Śraddhā*, "confidence"—often rendered as "faith"—is the first subject of the classical eightfold path leading the monk to enlightenment. Without trust in the Buddha's teachings, it was realized, no beginning could be made; no "right views" could be gained. Already in the first canonical writings *śraddhā* is often compared to a boat,[3] and hence the whole imagery of our text is not foreign. Moreover, Buddhism implies mysticism in its very structure. A little further on, Nāgārjuna quotes a verse which with minor variations occurs in various early texts. With the Buddha's own words, it speaks of the liberating force and the incomprehensibility of the Buddha's teachings. At the same time it seems to sum up the apparent paradox of all mysticism:

My Law is very difficult to grasp. It is capable of breaking the shackles. Men, bound to their cravings for the triple world, cannot understand it.[4]

It might also be admitted that what we recognized as "subjective reservedness" in the formal opening line of a *sūtra* finds a

2. After Lamotte, pp. 56–57.
3. See Lamotte, p. 56, n.2.
4. Lamotte, p. 59.

justification in Nāgārjuna's comments. The term was intended to indicate the mysterious character of conveying "religious knowledge." The *sūtras* presenting the Buddha's teachings conform to the style of many a myth in this respect, and Nāgārjuna's commentary, if anything, underlines the mystery of communication.

Nevertheless, neither the inner logic of Buddhist tradition nor an exposition of mythological characteristics tells the whole story. Nāgārjuna's philosophical style is not the style of myth, and his discovery of the whole complexity of *śraddhā* in the very first word of the *sūtra* is at least unusual. The tenacity of the mystical philosopher is most striking and makes both views inadequate.

The search for a deeper meaning is persevered in until the one opening word yields its secret: the first and fundamental insight for the Buddhist path of liberation. No doubt, the surprisingly new and expanded meaning simple words acquire is a matter of allegorization, yet the force of Nāgārjuna's reasonings amounts to *a new symbolism*. In order to gain some understanding of what happens to traditional data at the hands of a mystic, we should give full weight to the word perseverance.

We saw at the beginning of this discussion on myth and mysticism how religious experience is framed in a given mythology. With the mystic it is as if a new framework is created. That makes him different. His creative power reorganizes the "ordinary" data of his tradition. The mystic's experiences are not only "had," but *formed* in a simultaneously new framework of perception and understanding. Thus the mystic's perseverance is to be seen not only as the peculiar gift of an individual. It involves at the same time the power of creating symbols which affect the basic orientation, the mythology, of many men.

The flowering of Mahāyāna philosophy—of which Nāgārjuna

is an illustrious exponent—is related to the triumphal march of Buddhism over large parts of Asia. The great work of Nāgārjuna from which we quoted was not preserved in India, but has come to us through a Chinese translation. Of course, no single reason explains such a huge phenomenon as the expanse of Buddhism, but it is not difficult to see that the allegorical interpretation of texts helped a great deal. Textual details and Indian geographical particulars could be dealt with as matters that *had* to have a deeper meaning.

In this context one might think of missionary gimmicks or oversimplified teaching and preaching devices, when an infinite meaning is given to a specific place-name. Nevertheless, we should remember that unmistakable mystical forces were at work in the rejuvenation of the Buddhist teachings. It is a general human ability to make a mystical vision into a myth, a new creation into a cliché, a seer's interpretation into an exegetical gimmick, but in the daring interpretations by Nāgārjuna the initial force, capable of creating symbolisms, is tangible.

Sūtra: The Buddha resided in the city of Rājagṛha.
Śāstra: This sentence should now be explained.
Question: Why is it said that the Buddha resided in Rājagṛha, instead of giving a direct exposition of the teachings of the Prajñāpāramitā?
Answer: The author mentions place, time and persons so that people can have faith (śraddhā) in his account.[5]

Such interpretations were decisive in the course of history.

5. Lamotte, p. 162.

16 ✡
Myth
and
Mysticism

W E A R E as uninformed about man's first mystical experience as we are about his first myth. In the data we
have, we never find mystical documents in isolation,
but always together with a certain mythological background. Sociologically, this conclusion is self-evident.
Mystics are part of a human community; even if they
are among the intellectual elite, and if they go "beyond"
the tradition, they cannot very well bypass all societal
means of communication.

We cannot speak of *religion*—in the singular—
without having some understanding of religions—
various specific forms and traditions—and without

realizing that they are channeled through sociological configurations. The same thing is true for mysticism and the variety of its forms.

All this is no more than saying the obvious. For stripped of embellishments, it is no more than recognizing the fact that all societies have their intelligentsia. This conclusion does not illuminate the phenomena of mysticism.

A second sort of conclusion is equally obvious and would have been reached even more quickly if we had chosen to present the mystical data somewhat differently. We could have pinpointed mystical themes corresponding to the characteristic forms of myth we established. There is a close correspondence that is hard to overlook. The "dimming of opposites" in myth is paralleled in the peculiar character of mysticism which always looks paradoxical. In fact, the element of paradox in many a mystical document is much more striking than in the literary form of myth. Rāmānuja begins the treatise we referred to before with a hymn of praise to God (Viṣṇu) whom he calls at the same time "inaccessible for our words and thought (vāṅmanasayor abhūmiḥ)" and "the one who is the object of sight for people who bow to Him (natajanadṛśām bhūmiḥ)."[1]

Similarly, an "inverse effect" and a "subjective reservedness" could be demonstrated, for experiences of the infinite in the infinitely small and the mystery of gaining supreme wisdom abound. And the "grotesque"? Perhaps even grotesque elements could be shown to exist in some mystic visionary accounts, although here everyone would begin to feel some hesitancy.

I should feel reluctant to make very much of the similarity in

1. A. Hohenberger (trans.), *Rāmānuja's Vedāntadīpa*, p. XIII.

all instances. We have noted the seriousness of mystical concerns, and we should not forget it here. A likeness with the characteristics of myth exists, no doubt, but this literary conclusion conveys not much more than the sociological one. It reveals little of the nature of mysticism and its relation to myth. No matter how obvious the conclusion seems, it is greatly devaluated by the sensation we have in listening to the voices in the documents. As a rule, the myth fascinates us immediately. The mystical account hardly ever does; instead, it requires an effort of steady concentration. In addition to this sensation, there is something else that should prevent a thematic, over-all association of myth and mysticism. The further a mystical document is from ourselves, historically or geographically, the more it looks like myth. This can only mean that our subjectivity plays tricks on us, also when we think ourselves fairly sure of understanding the general relationship of myth and mysticism.

We saw how the mysticism in the Bhagavadgītā expressed itself by resuming and weaving together themes and ideas of an ancient religious heritage. To be sure, a new interpretation was presented, but the new experiences derived their force from clearly recognizable religious ideas and cultic practices of the earlier Brahmanic and Vedic past. Shamanic accounts of dreams and initiatory trials seem to conform to certain standard patterns in their respective societies. In fact, the accounts read like myths. In cultures that know shamans an important place is frequently given to the myth that narrates the origin of shamanism. In other words, a mythical model is given for the shamanic experience and techniques, and the narrative pattern is evident to any reader. The closer we get to a tradition that has affected our own views, the harder it is to identify "mythical" forms. For me, the difficulty arises with someone like Augustine or Nicholas of Cusa, whom we mentioned. The difficulty seems inescapable with a modern mystic like Thérèse de Lisieux (1873–1897). Of course, her relationship to the Christian tradition is beyond dispute; she was canonized in the Catholic church. Nevertheless, the account she herself gave of her spiritual progress makes the impression of a reflective auto-biography. Few words are spent on the climactic celebrations of the church. Everything of importance seems to be turned "inward" —perhaps the major reason why this saint could become so amaz-ingly popular in a world in which the "objective" data of the Christian tradition seemed to have dwindled. At any rate, an ac-count like hers, close to ourselves in time and in the "feel" of spiritual obstacles, makes it extraordinarily difficult to determine its traditionally "mythical" character. Apparently, a certain distance is necessary for the observer to come up with general conclusions associating mythological and mystical characteristics.

Are general conclusions impossible? On closer investigation, do they all depend on our subjectivity? It certainly seems almost impossible to say anything "objectively" and "in general" about matters that are particular by nature.

When the problem—or, if you will, the mystery—of subjectiv-ity arises, two ways are possible. The first is the way of repression. One can act as if the observer's subjectivity had nothing to do with it all and propound the "objective" conclusions with great aplomb. One should not be too hard on scholars who devote themselves to the study of myth or of mysticism and are tempted to follow this path. We are in need of sober scholarship that makes clear what "influences" are at work in this, that, or the other mystic. Espe-cially in the study of mysticism, such objective presentations of facts and themes can reveal undercurrents of thought that are of great significance to understand man in some civilizations and periods of which the more easily accessible facets, of politics, economics, and the arts, and philosophy, do not tell the whole story.

It should be clear however that in this small treatise on myth and mysticism a repression of our subjectivity cannot be useful. Treating of myth, we have not tried to outline "the history of myth." Instead, the examples of myths from different cultures and times have shown us the astounding variety in this type of literature. We have not tried to lump all these particularities and subjectivities of religious expression together in one "objective" overview. Instead, we have asked whether we knew of comparable expressions among ourselves. That means, we have consciously raised the question of our own subjectivity and its stylized expressions—in other words, our culture. Through forms of literature we were familiar with we could suggest characteristics of myth.

We purposely underlined the historical variety of mystical forms. This was necessary because of the misconception that all mysticism is the same thing. As with myth, the details count most. The characteristic details of mythical literature enabled us to speak of the freedom of man in myth. Speaking now of the relation between myth and mysticism, the only significant conclusions can be drawn within this perspective. This means not a repression of our subjectivity, but, to the extent possible, a recognition of it.

Conclusions about myth and mysticism that take the mythological dimension of man—as we understand it—into account, are much more difficult to draw than the relatively neat, "objective" conclusions we discussed.

A questioning attitude is part of our own mythology. It seems to be fostered in all places and on all levels and is not always striking in its profundity. Sometimes it seems a matter more of superstition than of an exacting search. But that it is cultivated— made into a cult—cannot be doubted. One could even say that a questioning attitude is accepted without question, and that is precisely what produces the mythical flavor. Every author who sends a manuscript to a publishing house receives a number of questions about the child of his brains from an editorial assistant who is paid for bringing forth these questions. In the mind of the editorial assistant is an image of the reading public whose (imagined) questions should be considered. No public dignitary, be he ever so low in rank, can fulfill his position without submitting himself to interviews with cultic regularity.

As scholars we accept the openness of all scholarly endeavors as a natural part of our world. We are reconciled to the fact that scientific results yield new problems and we are suspicious of premature solutions and scientific answers with "final" pretensions. In this climate, it is not so strange that disciplines of thought which center in "final" propositions—theology and metaphysics— are not particularly popular.

A word like "spiritual" has become suspect. Depth-psychologists, sociologists and others whose profession brings them into contact with man's "spiritual life" avoid such words. Our mythology then does not just insist on a questioning attitude; it seems to make puzzlement mandatory. In America we speak of a "pluralistic" society. A piece of sociological jargon, describing the multifarious groups of people and their ideologies and interests, has become a common word and helps to give a scientific (and hence acceptable) basis to our puzzlement about fundamental human orientations.

No matter how such puzzlement is dressed up or enforced,

it exists. The circumstance that all people know of it and are conscious of it one way or another may explain that mystical writings—not unlike myths—have come to enjoy a new popularity; some have found their way into pocketbooks. Here, I think, some degree of kinship really exists. Is not the mystic the person who dares to puzzle the whole way? This kinship certainly is far from an identity, but it may throw some light on a question that is often raised: Why do mystics who proclaim that the essence of their experience is ineffable and unknowable nevertheless speak of it? Nothing could be clearer than this in terms of the mythology of our time. "Puzzlement" may be a disrespectful word to use for venerable mystical treatises, yet it is evident that puzzlement *must* be expressed.

Puzzlement is part of human life. For long periods it may be dormant, but as soon as it rises to the surface, the mystic can hardly be ignored. The contradictions of human existence are his materials. His courage or talent to persevere until the very end and to realize and experience the final paradox can come to be accepted as a model in a time of questions. Martyrdom of course is not in conflict with this, but rather confirms his quality as model. The ruling mythology (which here certainly is not the same as the official theological systems) cannot fail to be affected.

The more serious the spirit of questioning is, the more of an impact is made by mystics, and, at the same time, the more people attain mystical experiences. It is interesting to observe that half of the selections in professor E. O'Brien's anthology of mystical writings come from the Renaissance period.

Of course, it would not be justified to deduce that mysticism is the sole inspiration for myth or for a mythical rejuvenation. But that it can provide a significant component in periods of general puzzlement—whatever its causes—seems undeniable.

Some periods and some traditions are more open to mysticism than others and it is not far-fetched to relate this openness to a willingness or an obsession to entertain questions. There is a mystical signature in all important religious texts in India, beginning with the late Vedic and post-Vedic period. We have seen something of its vocabulary, marked by a much greater psychological subtlety than Western thinkers were able to employ. The history of Indian civilization shows a continuous confrontation with religious traditions of local communities. History itself posed a variety of questions that had to be dealt with. The unity of the world presented itself as a new problem continually. The majority of confrontations took place with small communities. Fighting, also in the realm of doctrinal disputations, could not settle the problem. Religiously, mythological rejuvenations and incorporations occurred. Here too, not all new myths could become mystical treatises. But the nature of the questions made mystical influences almost natural. It is difficult to say what was first in time and in significance: the expansion of Indian culture both in its Buddhist and its Brahmanic and Hindu forms, or the precise vocabulary serving fundamental human questions. History shows them together, interdependent. Some of the most influential Indian schools of thought (especially Sāṃkhya and Yoga) speak of the nature and development of the world and man's inner structure and growth as complementary. Expressions of general cosmic symbolism and individual experience often coincide.

Instead of saying that some traditions are more open, one could as well say that some are more closed to mystical experiences.

As we saw, orthodox Islam, with its juridical structure, could persecute some of its mystics. Protestant Christianity, on the whole, has not been so kindly disposed toward its mystics. When Calvin created the office of the minister, his model was the prophet and scholar rather than the mystic. This choice is typical of an attitude in the reformed tradition which has consequences for the notion of myth. Clarity counts most; this clarity has its source in God's Word which in principle is the same for all. All church orders designed in the churches of the Reformation resist hierarchical divisions. Myths, which by nature are "polyinterpretable," and mystics, who are fundamentally "different" people, could not really fit in. It may be interesting to note that Calvin himself detested the writings of his contemporary Rabelais,[2] the same one who helped us in discerning features of mythological literature.

A few remarks like these about Calvin and the reformed tradition could not possibly exhaust the subject. A mythical propensity is constitutive of man. Likewise, with whatever variation and intensity, mystical ways reassert themselves in any tradition. Discussing the nature of Christian life, Calvin was not afraid to speak of a "mystical union" (*Institutes* III, 11, 10). This was not a matter of merely descriptive words. The continuous ethical and ascetic concerns of Calvin in all his writings are revealed in expressions that cannot be separated from mystical structures. Man's spiritual duty involves the victory over his desires for the world and his fear of death. The "mystical union" is a real experience. Needless to say, in the churches of the Reformation, next to the reflective concerns for a Christian existence, other elements such

2. Jacques LeClerq (trans.), *Rabelais: The Five Books of Gargantua and Pantagruel* (New York: Modern Library, n.d.), Introduction, pp. xxi–xxii.

as prayer life and the real presence of the Lord in the communion remained potential sources of mystical experience.

The questioning temper of our own time may be the major reason why we can understand something of the relation between myth and mystical urges, while only a generation ago the two were viewed as rather different subjects. Myth was generally seen as inadequate doctrinal formulation, and, until this very day, as a theoretical expression of an accepted social structure. Mysticism on the other hand was seen as originating in an evolved religious consciousness, a late phenomenon in the history of man. It is true, both of these views were adhered to with an array of facts and sophistication that one would hesitate to refute in all details. Nevertheless, our problem makes it possible and necessary to focus on something else. The variety of historical forms cannot be replaced by a scheme of evolution, and yet, it was in surveying multifarious mythical and mystical expressions that we took our refuge at times in notions with a theoretical, or even nonhistorical ring: the "mythological propensity" of man and the influence of a "mystical component." Such terms seemed necessary to me to be fair to the data of myths and mystics, and to prevent ourselves from dissolving them in an external scheme.

From the point of view of the masses in the tradition of a myth, the creation myth does not merely give a doctrinal exposition of the world's origin. No, it tells of a *transformation* of the ordinary worldly things which in their ordinariness become unbearable. Its dynamic, creative, and recreative function is borne out by the fact that a creation myth must be recited—or, to use the modern approximation, the fact that we must give a form to our human freedom. If we can legitimately speak of myth in this manner, the kinship to myth in any imaginable human situation becomes clearer too. If a "rebellious" element is essential to myth, it certainly is evident in mysticism. The mystical journeys beyond the accepted tradition can be said to extend the rebellion. Not only is there (as in the case of the shaman) the talent to *live* to symbolism which is a mere "ideogram" for the community, but sometimes the mystical experience and certitude constitute a rebellion against accepted dogma. At least in part, the wave of mystics in the Renaissance period can be understood as a reaction to a scholastic tradition. Not only the "ordinary" facts of life, suffering, and death can be felt as unbearable, but also the "standardized" images of God. Similar things can be said about Jewish and other forms of mysticism. In an individual experience, accepted dogmatic formulas can create the sensation of utter forlornness and have an impact on the manner in which a divine terror is felt.

Let me repeat that these statements about man's mythical and mystical dimensions are not meant to reduce the whole problem to one pattern. Historically, the sensations of the mystic are never expressed in such a manner as to nullify an earlier mythology. On the contrary, what is being said here is rather meant to show the meaning of the fact that we find only specific mystics in specific traditions. A mutual dependency exists in every case. It is not possible for the best of scholars to divide the whole world in two different groups: those with mythological minds in great variety on one hand and a homogeneous group of mystics on the other. The Christian visionary does not see Avalokiteśvara's heaven unless he has already been informed about it; a Hindu mystic does not see the Christian cross in the skies nor the virgin Mary, unless he has heard about them before. Our statements imply a relationship between religion in general and mysticism, but are not fit to suggest that the latter is the cause of the former. We saw that myths "transcend" or consciously ignore empirical and logical facts of life. In every tradition mystics realize the sense of myths all the way. They do so not only by repeating the myths but by breaking through the "last" pronouncements of myth.

One peculiarity in our "public" modern mythical complex makes it difficult to evaluate our inclination toward questioning and puzzling or to appreciate mysticism. This peculiarity may also have much to do with it that we do not like to think of ourselves as being in the spell of any mythology at all. It is the tremendous significance of youth. Our time may be full of questions, and for that reason alone an open mind for mystical accounts may exist, but it is only fair to add that the overwhelming majority of our questions are not full-grown. Not in the last place through the "mass media," an occupation with short-term questions and goals has become a regular feature of our common life. The "puzzlement" of the mystics whose memory history has found worth preserving is tangibly different. We have found that the mystic has the tenacity to make his puzzlement the beginning of his life's concern. Our own cult of questions may open our eyes to his "experiments," but the long breath of his quest cannot be easily identified with our endeavors. It is a truism to say in America that the standard is set by the young. It may not be true in fact, but it describes one feature of the "modern world" quite correctly. Changes in art and in politics are hailed because they bring in fresh blood or simply because they are "something new." It is not necessary to elaborate that the affectation of change develops its own stilted forms and often turns into a conservatism none of its devotees would like to face up to as his own.

All serious mystical documents are marked by a mature contemplation which is hardly ever the preoccupation of the young. There may be several reasons why Christian mystics have always had a preference for the gospel of John, but it could hardly be a coincidence that the author of the fourth gospel makes the impression of an elderly person because of his style and a certain repetitiousness very unlike that of a youth.

It follows that when we look for points of contact in our own times to understand the relation of myth and mysticism, we should pay attention particularly to puzzles of crucial importance. We have seen that mystical treatises are less "entertaining" than myths. Mystics, even when dealing with the same substance as narrators of myth, demonstrate a single-minded concentration that is never a common possession. Even in the light of a great many mythological traditions we look like people who suffer from youthful activity with our short-term questions and goals. How much more in the light of mystical writings and their maturity! The mystery of the perfect oneness or the expressions of perfect rest and stability, so prominent in the Indian texts, seem the opposite of our cultivated questionings. It takes a special effort to visualize anything *functioning* like that in "our mythology." Of course, I am still aware that no one is able to sum up the myth of his time, yet the youthful and continually shifting zeal of our time, making it especially hard to locate our central myth, makes it perhaps impossible to identify something that functions mystically.

With due respect to recently canonized saints, it seems to me that another type of man, less "officially" religious, is most illustrative. I am thinking of the true and dedicated scientist, the monk of modern life. I am far from suggesting that every modern scientist is a mystic. The emphasis is on the true and dedicated scientist, and I realize quite well that his features are more conspicuously monkish than mystical. To avoid misunderstanding, I should stress that this choice is not meant to disqualify the mystics of any clearly recognizable religious tradition today—if such a thing were possible. I choose the example only as an illustration of a mystic-like phenomenon in our own time, viewed from a mythology in *statu nascendi*.

There is, however, no lack of encouragement in the history of religion to place the true modern scientist side by side with the mystic. In the preceding pages we drew the figure of the shaman into our discussion. He too, in spite of his mystical experiences and function with respect to myth, cannot be easily labeled. In so far as he is an expert in curing the sick and has first-hand knowledge about the structure of the universe, he encompasses what in modern parlance would be very different specializations, including that of the theoretical physicist. We have mentioned Nicholas of Cusa's mathematical interests. Many of the problems discussed in Indian mystical texts are common to various schools of thought and rise not only from some supreme experience but from a scientific concern at the same time; among them are "the atom theory, relation between cause and effect, whole and parts, agent and action, etc."[3]

In an address honoring Max Planck,[4] Albert Einstein spoke in his lucid way about the work of the natural scientist next to that of the poet, the painter, and the speculative philosopher. Among the motives leading men to art and science is in Einstein's as in Schopenhauer's view "escape from everyday life with its

3. Richard H. Robinson, *op. cit.*, p. 70.
4. Albert Einstein (trans. Alan Harris), *Essays in Science* (New York: Philosophical Library, n.d.), pp. 1–5.

painful crudity and hopeless dreariness, from the fetters of one's own ever-shifting desires." But another motive is more significant in Einstein's thought. He calls it a "personal" one, but it clearly surpasses all ideas of an individual's selfish desires. It is something a historian of religions would understand immediately as a symbolism of orientation, and, we may add, its mystical quality is unmistakable:

Man tries to make for himself in the fashion that suits him best a simplified and intelligible picture of the world; he then tries to some extent to substitute this cosmos of his for the world of experience, and thus to overcome it. This is what the painter, the poet, the speculative philosopher, and the natural scientist do, each in his own fashion. He makes this cosmos and its construction the pivot of his emotional life, in order to find in this way the peace and security which he cannot find in the narrow whirlpool of personal experience.

Einstein's principal concern in his address is of course the image of the theoretical physicist. The fashion of the theoretical physicist is characterized by "the highest possible standard of rigorous precision in the description of relations, such as only the use of mathematical language can give." But, Einstein continues, a method of this type and the application of such standards are bought at a price: "Supreme purity, clarity and certainty at the cost of completeness." But no matter how small a part of nature can be studied in this manner, the outcome must be "called by the proud name of a theory of the Universe," for fundamentally, Einstein argues, the theory is meant to be such as to allow a deduction of the laws governing all natural processes. "The supreme task of the physicist is to arrive at those universal elementary laws from which the cosmos can be built up by pure deduction." The similarity to the speculative philosopher which fascinates Einstein could not be expressed more precisely. In the same context, Einstein speaks of a longing for "what Leibnitz described so happily as a 'pre-established harmony.'" Is it far-fetched to think back to the function of creation myths? Still, it seems to me that the closest kinship exists between the ideal theoretical physicist—who are always few, Einstein emphasizes—and the mystic. Speaking about the universal elementary laws the physicist tries to arrive at, Einstein adds in the next sentence: "There is no logical path to these laws; only intuition, resting on sympathetic understanding of experience, can reach them." Almost at the end of his address, he says that "The state of mind which enables a man to do work of this kind is akin to that of the religious worshipper or the lover. . . ."

Some notes on the limitation and use of a comparison between the devoted theoretical physicist and the mystic seem in order and may help in our own historical situation to illuminate and summarize our views. Einstein is well aware of it that with theories of the universe "evolution has shown that at any given moment, out of all conceivable constructions, a single one has always proved itself absolutely superior to the rest." To be sure, no simple notion of progress is implied here, for theoretically arguments may exist in favor of various systems. Yet the victories of successive theories of the universe approximate a sort of evolution that we could not meaningfully use in the subject of mysticism.

In recent times, theoretical physics has been accompanied by technological advances. In the realm of mysticism, there is nothing similar to suggest evolution. Even more generally, as we have seen before, it is rather misleading to speak of an evolution of religious consciousness. If in the history of religious symbolism and its experiences some instance of progress occurs, it could hardly be registered as unambiguously as in the technical results of scientific theories. It may be that here or there the disposal of the dead by returning them to "the eternal potentiality" of the waters led to the invention of boats for transport of the living. It can very well be imagined, but examples of this sort do not convey the idea of results proper to the notion of evolution. Moreover, such examples are also too particular to carry much weight for a dreamer or expounder of religious evolution.

Human situations—the only ones in which we find myths and mystics—are historical situations and always complex. We should not call them stages in an evolution without immediately imposing limitations on ourselves. "Stages in an evolution" are allegory in a study of man. They have a useful function only with respect to clearly defined topics: the history of seafaring, a marketing system, or property rights. It is true of course that in religious matters also we discern certain sequences. A clear instance is monotheism, which always follows polytheism (as in Israel and Islam). But then too, one could not very well say that one step necessarily led to the next; the historical variety is too great, and in too many cases the next step was not taken at all, or was altogether different. It would clearly be absurd to claim that monotheism meant progress.

We have seen evidence in abundance that mystics do not express themselves in the same terms in different cultures and cultural phases. No one could launch an "objective" statement to the effect that Ignatius of Loyola improved on the Pseudo-

Dionysius. But in all cases, in all human situations, the mystic does show his urge for a simplicity beyond the whirlpool of personal existences. Obviously, he does not aim for enjoyment but for something imposing its validity on the plurality he knows more incisively than we know, even in our most mythological knowledge.

That urge for validity makes the comparison with Einstein's ideal scientist illuminating. This type enjoys an unequaled esteem by all whose lives are shaped in the mythological quests of our time. Here are some people, it is felt, who have that single-minded attention that can identify the important questions in man's puzzlement about his universe. Moreover, the answers they present are authoritative, without becoming definitive, as seemed the questions and answers of the catechisms that sank into oblivion. In other words, the scientist is not merely a modern illustration of the phenomenon of mysticism; he is felt to be the ideal man in the perspective of our common and peculiar questioning temper. Hence he illustrates equally well the influence of mysticism on the formation of myths.

A final word about the attainability of mystical certainties may not be out of order, because of the wave of cravings for inner experiences today. Einstein's portrayal of the dedicated scientist has already set the tone for these concluding remarks.

I am not thinking in the first place of the "consciousness-expanding" drugs that have stirred so many minds—directly, the minds of those who have taken them and indirectly the minds of the many who fear them. Before these things happened, before the fad of hippies and before the desires for instant mysticism took on such proportions, one could hear statements such as the following by a scholarly church dignitary: "There is considerable expectation that we are on the verge of a considerable spread of mysticism among men in ordinary walks of life."[5]

A spiritual climate that favors cravings for mystical experiences does not by that token produce mysticism, while a proselytizing mysticism is almost a contradiction in terms. Characteristic of mysticism is concentration on mythological data. Even when transcending these data, it does not ignore them, nor reject them, nor replace them by something else. Its intuition is never the same as an uncritical attitude. It does not revel in some random symbolisms that appeal to an individual taste, and—should it be repeated?—one can never define its goal blankly as happiness.

The main problem of understanding the nature of popular mysticism and the generalizations made about it is old. It is the problem of mysticism *and gnosticism* on which we touched in speaking of Plotinus. For Plotinus, the world-view of the gnostics and their schemes of self-realization were not in accordance with Plato,[6] and that alone condemned them. It amounted to a condemnation. The opposition between the two is not sufficiently explained by distinguishing their doctrinal formulations, such as a tendency toward "superintellectualism" or monism among certain mystics and a tendency toward dualism (matter as evil and radically different from the supreme spiritual good) among gnostics. In modern terms we could very well say that in the eyes of the mystics the gnostic teachings appeared "gimmicky." A certain inarticulateness offended the mystic philosopher, and so did the arrogance

5. William Quinlan Lash, Bishop of Bombay, "Christian Mysticism," in S. Radhakrishnan a.o., *History of Philosophy Eastern and Western* (London: Allen & Unwin, 1953), p. 197.

6. Norden, *op. cit.*, p. 85, n.1. See also p. 193.

implied in gnostic claims. In this vein Plotinus gave his criticism (in Enneads II, 9, 9).[7] He speaks there of the "dream-flight" which prevents a man from attaining the identity of which his soul is capable, and the stupidity of people fancying themselves to rise above the "Intellectual-Principle," which in his own mysticism plays such a crucial role. Likewise in India, a tension between mystics and gnostics has often been manifest, although the two had most of their vocabulary in common. Many of Śaṃkara's and Rāmānuja's followers were suspicious of the Tāntrikas for whom "instant liberation" was more than a figure of speech. No matter how our present-day mythology of questions may induce one to think of a widely divulged mysticism, mystics remain an aristocracy in religious affairs.

The only possible sort of wider distribution of mystical notions involves a change. Propagated mysticism becomes gnosticism at best, or, at worst, a chaotic superstitiousness. Students who have devoted themselves in recent years to unraveling the history of the gnostic movement in late antiquity have in their way confirmed Plotinus' judgment. "Of gnosis," one of them said, "our knowledge is sufficient to say confidently: the number of duffers and muddle-heads here surpasses those elsewhere . . ."[8]

Whoever would draw on this association with earlier gnostics to formulate with confidence his own condemnation of all recent hankerers after inner experience would do wrong. He should remember that these recent forms of popular mysticism—even if this word is improperly applied—depend on the mythology of our age. This mythology includes emphatically the acceptance of

7. See also Norden, p. 193.
8. G. Quispel, "De heidense gnosis" in J. Waszink a.o. (eds.), *Het oudste Christendom en de antieke cultuur* (Haarlem: Tjeenk Willink, 1951), I, 152.

constant questions and the problems of brief satisfactions with short-term goals; its cults enforce continuous modifications and the rejection of everything that might seem to be a spiritual authority. In other words, we are lacking the means and the patience to face up to the enigma of formulating our freedom. Perhaps in some later time it will be viewed as a grandiose process of repression. These points must be fully realized before one can evaluate or pass a judgment on the exuberant interest in inner experiences. It may be true that the rejection of the comforts of our society does not come off well in comparison to the mystic's dark night of the soul, but neither would our mythology in comparison to the mythology behind St. John of the Cross.

Many years ago, Berdyaev told the story of a student from Soviet Russia who had come to Paris. When he was about to return he was asked whether he was not sorry to go back. He surprised his questioners by saying what they least expected, for he claimed that there was one thing he had missed especially during his stay in the West: freedom. The misunderstanding is transparent. In the estimation of the young student it was precisely a lack of freedom which made one government tumble after another. Constant modification could not be a worthy enterprise and certainly not an expression of freedom. There is a grain of truth in the journalistic reports that compare the drug-addiction of today with the function Communist party membership had for many a generation ago.

More important than these similes is the realization that present cravings for mystical experience cannot be understood without the background of our present myths. We should conclude that objections to the former cannot mean much without drastically changing the latter. But how should one begin to change a mythology that affects all of us in its sweep? The work of a historian of religion has its limits. To spell out (which is still not the same as to bring about) where our mythology should go should be the task of a philosopher, who may be affected too, but has not bowed his knees before the short-term questions of our present-day imagination.

Appendix

Rāmāyaṇa I, 45, 15ff.
Translated into English verse
by Ralph T. H. Griffith.

'List, Rama, list, with closest heed
The tale of Indra's wondrous deed,
And mark me as I truly tell
What here in ancient days befell.
Ere Krita's famous Age had fled,
Strong were the sons of Diti bred;
And Aditi's brave children too
Were very mighty, good and true.
The rival brothers fierce and bold
Were sons of Kasyap lofty-souled.
Of sister mothers born, they vied,
Brood against brood, in jealous pride.

Once, as they say, band met with band,
And, joined in awful council, planned
To live, unharmed by age and time,
Immortal in their youthful prime.
Then this was, after due debate
The counsel of the wise and great,
To churn with might the milky sea
The life-bestowing drink to free.
This planned, they seized the Serpent King,
Vasuki, for their churning-string,
And Mandar's mountain for their pole,
And churned with all their heart and soul.
As thus, a thousand seasons through,
This way and that the snake they drew,
Biting the rocks, each tortured head
A very deadly venom shed.
Thence, bursting like a mighty flame,
A pestilential poison came,
Consuming, as it onward ran,
The home of God, and fiend, and man.
Then all the suppliant Gods in fear
To Sandar, mighty lord, drew near.
To Rudra, King of Herds, dismayed, 'Save
'Save us, O save us, Lord!' they prayed.
Then Viṣṇu, bearing shell, and mace,
And discus, showed his radiant face,
And thus addressed in smiling glee
The Trident-wielding deity:
What treasure first the Gods upturn
From troubled Ocean, as they churn,

Should—for thou art the eldest—be
Conferred, O best of Gods, on thee.
Then come, and for thy birthright's sake,
This venom as thy firstfruits take.'
He spoke, and vanished from their sight,
Śiva saw their wild affright,
And heard his speech by whom is borne
The mighty bow of bending horn,
The poisoned flood at once he quaffed
As 'twere the Amrit's heavenly draught.
Then from the Gods departing went
Śiva, the lord pre-eminent.
The host of Gods and Asurs still
Kept churning with one heart and will.
But Mandar's mountain, whirling round,
Pierced to the depths below the ground.
Then Gods and bards in terror flew
To him who mighty Madhu slew.
'Help of all beings! more than all,
The Gods on thee for aid may call.
Ward off, O mighty-armed! our fate,
And bear up Mandar's threatening weight.'
Then Vishṇu, as their need was sore,
The semblance of a tortoise wore,
And in the bed of Ocean lay
The mountain on his back to stay.
Then he, the soul pervading all,
Whose locks in radiant tresses fall,
One mighty arm extended still,
And grasped the summit of the hill.

And Asurs are the Titan crowd
Her gentle claims who disallowed,
Then from the foamy sea was freed
Uchchaihsravas, the generous steed,
And Kaustubha, of gems the gem,
And Soma, Moon God, after them.
    At length when many a year had fled,
Up floated, on her lotus bed,
A maiden fair and tender-eyed,
In the young flush of beauty's pride.
She shone with pearl and golden sheen,
And seals of glory stamped her queen.
On each round arm glowed many a gem,
On her smooth brows, a diadem.
Rolling in waves beneath her crown
The glory of her hair flowed down.
Pearls on her neck of price untold,
The lady shone like burnisht gold.
Queen of the Gods, she leapt to land,
A lotus in her perfect hand,
And fondly, of the lotus-sprung,
To lotus-bearing Vishnu clung.
Her Gods above and men below
As Beauty's Queen and Fortune know.
Gods, Titans, and the minstrel train
Still churned and wrought the troubled main.
So ranged among the Immortals, he
Joined in the churning of the sea.
    A thousand years had reached their close.
When calmly from the ocean rose

The gentle sage with staff and can,
Lord of the art of healing man.
Then as the waters foamed and boiled,
As churning still the Immortals toiled,
Forth sixty million fair ones came.
Born of the foam and water, these
Were aptly named Apsarases.
Each had her maids. The tongue would fail—
So vast the throng—to count the tale.
But when no God or Titan wooed
A wife from all that multitude,
Refused by all, they gave their love
In common to the Gods above.
Then from the sea still vext and wild
Rose Sura, Varun's maiden child.
A fitting match she sought to find:
But Diti's sons her love declined,
Their kinsmen of the rival brood
To the pure maid in honour sued.
Hence those who loved that nymph so fair
The hallowed name of Suras bear.
At length the prize so madly sought,
The Amrit, to their sight was brought.
For the rich spoil, 'twixt these and those
A fratricidal war arose,
And, host 'gainst host in battle, set,
Aditi's sons and Diti's met.
United, with the giants' aid,
Their fierce attack the Titans made,
And wildly raged for many a day

That universe-astounding fray.
When wearied arms were faint to strike,
And ruin threatened all alike,
Vishṇu, with art's illusive aid,
The Amrit from their sight conveyed.
That Best of Beings smote his foes
Who dared his deathless arm oppose:
Yea, Vishṇu, all-pervading God,
Beneath his feet the Titans trod.
Aditi's race, the sons of light,
Slew Diti's brood in cruel fight.
Then town-destroying Indra gained
His empire, and in glory reigned
O'er the three worlds, with bard and sage
Rejoicing in his heritage.

From *The Ramayan of Valmiki*, translated into English verse by Ralph T. H. Griffith. Reprint, with a memoir by M. N. Venkataswami, *Chowkhamba Sanskrit Studies*, Vol. XXIX (Varanasi: Chowkhamba, 1963, pp. 56–58).

Index

Absolute, the, 126. *See also* Brahman

Al-Halladj, 144

Allegorization, allegory: in mysticism, 159; in Nāgārjuna, 161–163. *See also* Nicholas of Cusa, 132–134; Eckhart, 145.

Amṛta, 68. *See also* Churning of the Ocean, translation of text.

Andersen, J. C., 147n

Andreus, Hans, 59–60

Apsaras, 74–75. *See also* Churning of the Ocean, translation of text.

Arberry, A. J., 125n

Arjuna, 135, 137

Augustine: uses language of (neo) Platonism, 121; and mysticism in Europe, 124; quoted by Cusanus, 133; universality in, 152–153; mystical experience of light, 157; mentioned, 98, 130, 166

Authority: of myth, 58, 90, 93; of the mystic's experiences, 111; scriptural, 142; religious, 144; divine, 157; spiritual, 184

Avyakta, 135–139 *passim*

Āyurveda, 80n

Beginning (the), beginnings: in myth, 16, 18, 19; in mysticism, 21, 132–134

Berdyaev, N., 184

Bhagavadgītā, 134–139 *passim*; 166

Bhāgavatapurāṇa, 46n, 53n, 55n, 56n

Boccasino, Renato, 115n

Boehme, Jacob, 45, 51–52

Brahman, 126, 142, 143

Brahmin: slaying of a, 53

Bṛhadāraṇyaka Upaniṣad, 107n

Buddha, 59, 108, 153, 160–163 *passim*

Buddhism, 161–163

Buddhist sūtras, 59, 160–163

Buitenen, J. A. B. van, 58n

Cakravartin, 108

Calvin, John, 172

Ceremony, 84, 85

Cervantes, 71–72

Churning of the Ocean: 73–77; "dimming the opposites" in, 46; "inverse effect" in, 54–56; the grotesque in, 67–69; "subjective reservedness" in, 76; literal translation of text, 78–82; poetic rendering, *see* Appendix; mentioned, 46

Clairvaux, Bernard of, 145

Coincidentia oppositorum: 24, 53; in Cusanus, 134

Coleridge, S. T., 65–66

Communion celebration, 136, 173

Confidence: concept in Buddhism, 160, 161. *See also* Śraddhā

Consciousness-expanding drugs, 181

Corbishley, T., 114n

Cosmogonic myth: usages of, 15–17, 22, 24, 47–49; is fundamental type, 15,